TeamCity 7 Continuous Integration Essentials

A step-by-step introductory tutorial and intelligible practical guide to successfully applying Continuous Integration via TeamCity

Volodymyr Melymuka

BIRMINGHAM - MUMBAI

TeamCity 7 Continuous Integration Essentials

Copyright © 2012 Packt Publishing

All rights reserved. No part of this book may be reproduced, stored in a retrieval system, or transmitted in any form or by any means, without the prior written permission of the publisher, except in the case of brief quotations embedded in critical articles or reviews.

Every effort has been made in the preparation of this book to ensure the accuracy of the information presented. However, the information contained in this book is sold without warranty, either express or implied. Neither the author, nor Packt Publishing, and its dealers and distributors will be held liable for any damages caused or alleged to be caused directly or indirectly by this book.

Packt Publishing has endeavored to provide trademark information about all of the companies and products mentioned in this book by the appropriate use of capitals. However, Packt Publishing cannot guarantee the accuracy of this information.

First published: December 2012

Production Reference: 1191212

Published by Packt Publishing Ltd.
Livery Place
35 Livery Street
Birmingham B3 2PB, UK.

ISBN 978-1-84969-376-9

www.packtpub.com

Cover Image by Rakesh Shejwal (shejwal.rakesh@gmail.com)

Credits

Author
Volodymyr Melymuka

Reviewer
Rickard Nilsson

Acquisition Editor
Kartikey Pandey

Commissioning Editors
Harsha Bharwani
Meeta Rajani
Priyanka Shah

Technical Editor
Charmaine Pereira

Copy Editor
Vrinda Amberkar

Project Coordinator
Shraddha Bagadia

Proofreader
Stephen Swaney

Indexer
Hemangini Bari

Graphics
Aditi Gajjar

Production Coordinator
Melwyn D'sa

Cover Work
Melwyn D'sa

About the Author

Volodymyr Melymuka is an agile and experienced Lead Software Engineer and a qualified team leader, who applies Continuous Integration with TeamCity for more than 4 years as of now. He took up key roles and led several projects in which he applied various agile/XP practices such as TDD, BDD, and continuous delivery, among others. During his work he used and administered many CI servers, namely TeamCity, Jenkins, and Bamboo. He currently works as a scrum master and team leader in TomTom's offshore development team.

His former working experience involved large enterprises such as UBS Investment Bank and BAWAG P.S.K., and a great unbelievable project for SecondMarket Inc. He has a number of professional certifications such as Certified ScrumMaster from Scrum Alliance and ICAgile Associate by ICAgile consortium.

Besides being interested in the latest web technologies and many others things, he is also a former musician and he is fond of portrait photography, especially the ones involving children.

> I want to thank everyone who in any way helped make this book happen. I am grateful to Packt Publishing for their offer to write this book. I appreciate all the efforts of Desmond Lownds, a Software Architect from Secondmarket Inc., spent in developing good software development skills in me. I send best wishes to Brendan Boyle, my manager at UBS Investment Bank for his assistance provided when I introduced scrum from scratch for an ongoing project. And of course, the biggest praise I would give is to my lovely wife Tetiana Gozha and our two beautiful daughters, Zoryana and Solomiya, for their infinite patience and reliable support throughout the countless hours they spent beside me during my work, and all my life.

About the Reviewer

Rickard Nilsson is a Software Architect, Developer, Craftsman, and an agile enthusiast with experience in a great variety of business applications ranging from e-commerce to intranet solutions. He holds a Master of Science degree in Information Technology.

Rickard has been a Continuous Integration practitioner and enthusiast for several years, implementing the practice in his own team as well as helping other teams in getting started with the process using tools such as TeamCity and Team Foundation Server. He has also been talking, writing blog posts, and answering questions on Stack Overflow (stackoverflow.com/) about Continuous Integration and related topics.

Rickard works as a consultant at Ninetech, a company providing expertise and solutions in digital market communication and IT. In his spare time, Rickard is a blogger at http://rickardnilsson.net.

The other books that Rickard has been involved in include *Continuous Integration in .NET*, Kawalerowicz and Berntson, and *The Art of Unit Testing, Second Edition*, Roy Osherove.

www.PacktPub.com

Support files, eBooks, discount offers and more

You might want to visit `www.PacktPub.com` for support files and downloads related to your book.

Did you know that Packt offers eBook versions of every book published, with PDF and ePub files available? You can upgrade to the eBook version at `www.PacktPub.com` and as a print book customer, you are entitled to a discount on the eBook copy. Get in touch with us at `service@packtpub.com` for more details.

At `www.PacktPub.com`, you can also read a collection of free technical articles, sign up for a range of free newsletters and receive exclusive discounts and offers on Packt books and eBooks.

`http://PacktLib.PacktPub.com`

Do you need instant solutions to your IT questions? PacktLib is Packt's online digital book library. Here, you can access, read and search across Packt's entire library of books.

Why Subscribe?
- Fully searchable across every book published by Packt
- Copy and paste, print and bookmark content
- On demand and accessible via web browser

Free Access for Packt account holders

If you have an account with Packt at `www.PacktPub.com`, you can use this to access PacktLib today and view nine entirely free books. Simply use your login credentials for immediate access.

Table of Contents

Preface	**1**
Chapter 1: Getting Started with TeamCity	**7**
Continuous integration	**8**
Features	**8**
Automatic and manual build triggering	8
Pre-tested commit	9
Instant notifications	9
Code coverage and inspections	9
Easy to verify code changes	9
Configurable test reports	9
Comprehensive build infrastructure	9
Enhanced VCS integration	10
Advanced features	10
Terms and concepts	**10**
Build agent	10
Build artifact	11
Build configuration	11
Code coverage	12
My Changes	12
Notifiers	13
Pre-tested commit (remote run)	13
Project	13
Version Control System	13
Architecture	**14**
Build lifecycle	**14**
Scheduling to a build agent	15
VCS specifics	16

Server-side checkout	16
Agent-side checkout	16
Running the build	16
Summary	**17**
Chapter 2: Sample Project	**19**
Creating the development environment	**20**
Installing JDK	20
Configuring your Windows environment	20
Installing Maven	22
Creating a sample project	**23**
Generating source by Maven	23
Installing IntelliJ IDEA	24
Opening your project with IDEA	**24**
Adding unit tests	**29**
Creating some testable code	29
Writing your first test	30
Launching our application	**32**
Summary	**33**
Chapter 3: Preparing a Continuous Integration Environment	**35**
Hardware requirements	**35**
Build agent	35
Server	36
Installing TeamCity server	**37**
Installing the Windows distribution	37
Installing the Linux multi-platform distribution	39
Installing from the WAR archive	42
Installing the build agent	**42**
Installing a default build agent	42
Running the TeamCity server	**44**
Summary	**46**
Chapter 4: Configuring the TeamCity Server	**47**
Prerequisites	**47**
Working with projects and build configurations	**49**
Creating a project	49
Creating a build configuration	50
Running the build configuration	52
Triggering builds automatically	53

Configuring and maintaining the TeamCity server	**57**
Project-related settings	57
Integrations	58
Server administration	58
Maintaining users and their permissions	**59**
Configuring notifications	**62**
E-mail	62
IDE	62
Windows tray	62
Jabber/XMPP	63
Atom/RSS feed	63
Already preinstalled configurations	63
Adding custom notification rules	63
Summary	**64**
Chapter 5: Integration with an IDE	**65**
IntelliJ IDEA	**65**
Installing from the plugins repository	66
Installing from the TeamCity server	66
Integration in action	**68**
IntelliJ IDEA	68
Eclipse	70
Summary	**72**
Chapter 6: Enhanced Techniques	**73**
Remote run	**73**
IntelliJ IDEA	75
Eclipse	80
Organizing multiple projects with templates	**84**
Copying the project	84
Update build configurations	86
Extracting and applying a template	87
Multi-step builds	**88**
Summary	**92**
Chapter 7: Advanced Configuration	**93**
User and group notifications	**93**
Upgrading to a newer version	**98**
Backup	99
Upgrading on Windows	100
Upgrading on Linux	101
Restoring	102

Advanced server settings	**102**
Installing an additional build agent	103
Assigning a dedicated build configuration	107
Summary	**108**
Appendix: Where to Go Next	**109**
Index	**111**

Preface

Nowadays, Agile application development is usually done at a fast pace when many developers are working on the same piece of code. Every so often, this becomes a real challenge if there's no permanent control over consistency of the project source. It is often impossible to force lazy and/or busy programmers to execute tests before and after each of their commits. Continuous Integration is a well-known lifesaver for distributed development environments, with TeamCity being one of the best and easy-to-use instruments utilizing it.

TeamCity 7 Continuous Integration Essentials is the first book of its kind that shows, in a sequential approach, how to implement Continuous Integration over generic projects and also encloses rich features of TeamCity as the project gradually evolves.

Learn how to do a quick start with TeamCity and suit most of the common needs right out of the box. As the project grows and more sophisticated requirements for the build process arise, the examples from this guide will assist you, showing how to unleash TeamCity's hidden powers and adjust advanced features to bring stability to the distributed development process.

You will learn how to start a new Java project from scratch, generating a working "skeleton" of a web application using Apache Maven, and later adding some business logic and writing certain tests. After that, you will know how to perform a swift attach of TeamCity facilities to your project and eventually change it into a rich-featured information source describing the current state of your venture. If you want to be benefitted from Continuous Integration and are considering using TeamCity, then this book is for you.

You will be acquainted with everything you need to know in order to apply Continuous Integration with TeamCity by installing it first, then turning on automatic supervision over your project's reliability, and finally tuning up advanced settings in order to match your needs.

What this book covers

Chapter 1, *Getting Started with TeamCity*, provides a brief overview of what TeamCity is, and which features make it so special. We'll learn its basic terms and concepts, main architecture, and build lifecycle.

Chapter 2, *Sample Project*, shows how to prepare your development environment, create a basic web application with Apache Maven, and finally launch it.

Chapter 3, *Preparing a Continuous Integration Environment*, describes the installation and basic setup of the TeamCity server and build agent bundle.

Chapter 4, *Configuring the TeamCity Server*, deals with creating a build configuration for a given project, setting up an automatic build triggering, and configuring personal notifications for user.

Chapter 5, *Integration with an IDE*, looks at installation of TeamCity integration plugin into IntelliJ IDEA and Eclipse. Also it is shown how useful this plugin could be in your daily work.

Chapter 6, *Enhanced Techniques*, examines some advanced TeamCity features like remote run and creation of build chains with dependent multi-step builds.

Chapter 7, *Advanced Configuration*, covers an upgrading routine together with a backup and restore process. You'll know how to create users and groups, install and connect additional build agent, and assign to an agent a particular build configuration.

Appendix, *Where to Go Next*, gives you some references for obtaining additional information on TeamCity.

What you need for this book

To try examples from this book yourself, you will need the Java software development kit with a version equal to or greater than 1.6 installed on Windows, Linux, or Mac OS X machine. Also, some version control system is needed, which could be any of the ones currently in the market. The sample project will be built by Apache Maven with a version not older than 2. To write code, it would be good to use a modern IDE such as Eclipse or IntelliJ IDEA.

Who this book is for

This book is great for developers willing to start utilizing Continuous Integration on a daily basis and it does not really matter how experienced you are at your programming skills. You may not need to be a programmer at all in order to use all the advantages of TeamCity. Quality Assurance engineers would benefit from this book as there's enough information explaining how to maintain a build configuration for tests and administer the TeamCity server. Even project managers and other managerial staff who don't actually work with code will find use for TeamCity as they will be kept abreast of a project's current status.

Conventions

In this book, you will find a number of styles of text that distinguish between different kinds of information. Here are some examples of these styles, and an explanation of their meaning.

Code words in text are shown as follows: "Choose the home of the project as working directory and enter `jetty:run`".

A block of code is set as follows:

```
package com.packtpub;
public class Calculator {
    public int sum(int x, int y) {
        return x + y;
    }
    public int multiply(int x, int y) {
        return x + y;
    }
}
```

When we wish to draw your attention to a particular part of a code block, the relevant lines or items are set in bold:

```
package com.packtpub;
public class Calculator {
    public int sum(int x, int y) {
        return x + y;
    }
    public int multiply(int x, int y) {
        return x + y;
    }
}
```

Any command-line input or output is written as follows:

```
[root@host]# wget http://download-ln.jetbrains.com/teamcity/TeamCity-
   7.0.2.tar.gz
```

New terms and **important words** are shown in bold. Words that you see on the screen, in menus or dialog boxes for example, appear in the text like this: " At any time we can schedule a manual build by simply clicking on the **Run** button.".

> Warnings or important notes appear in a box like this.

> Tips and tricks appear like this.

Reader feedback

Feedback from our readers is always welcome. Let us know what you think about this book—what you liked or may have disliked. Reader feedback is important for us to develop titles that you really get the most out of.

To send us general feedback, simply send an e-mail to feedback@packtpub.com, and mention the book title via the subject of your message.

If there is a topic that you have expertise in and you are interested in either writing or contributing to a book, see our author guide on www.packtpub.com/authors.

Customer support

Now that you are the proud owner of a Packt book, we have a number of things to help you to get the most from your purchase.

Downloading the example code

You can download the example code files for all Packt books you have purchased from your account at http://www.PacktPub.com. If you purchased this book elsewhere, you can visit http://www.PacktPub.com/support and register to have the files e-mailed directly to you.

Errata

Although we have taken every care to ensure the accuracy of our content, mistakes do happen. If you find a mistake in one of our books—maybe a mistake in the text or the code—we would be grateful if you would report this to us. By doing so, you can save other readers from frustration and help us improve subsequent versions of this book. If you find any errata, please report them by visiting http://www.packtpub.com/support, selecting your book, clicking on the **errata submission form** link, and entering the details of your errata. Once your errata are verified, your submission will be accepted and the errata will be uploaded on our website, or added to any list of existing errata, under the Errata section of that title. Any existing errata can be viewed by selecting your title from http://www.packtpub.com/support.

Piracy

Piracy of copyright material on the Internet is an ongoing problem across all media. At Packt, we take the protection of our copyright and licenses very seriously. If you come across any illegal copies of our works, in any form, on the Internet, please provide us with the location address or website name immediately so that we can pursue a remedy.

Please contact us at copyright@packtpub.com with a link to the suspected pirated material.

We appreciate your help in protecting our authors, and our ability to bring you valuable content.

Questions

You can contact us at questions@packtpub.com if you are having a problem with any aspect of the book, and we will do our best to address it.

Getting Started with TeamCity

The total number of software programs and applications being developed at the present time has never been greater and their scope has never been wider. Moreover, it still grows both in terms of increasing demand of getting every kind of business you need to have today or would need to be having tomorrow. All related new features should be introduced rapidly enough to leave competitors behind.

But speed comes at a well-known cost—you either make it quickly or of high quality. There are several possible ways to try to achieve both together, and TeamCity provides one of the best options to do that via Continuous Integration.

TeamCity is a very light instrument, easy to install, integrate, and maintain. It's a tool which helps you ensure that your software project not only compiles properly but can be assembled and (ideally) allowed to be delivered to operational destination production servers merely by glancing at the TeamCity welcome page. For distributed teams, it could give a priceless experience of having reliable codebase free from some forgotten to be committed source files and resources.

In this chapter we shall cover the following topics:

- Features
- Terms and concepts
- Architecture
- Build lifecycle

Continuous Integration

Continuous Integration is defined by Martin Fowler as follows:

> *Continuous Integration is a software development practice where members of a team integrate their work frequently; usually each person integrates at least daily – leading to multiple integrations per day. Each integration is verified by an automated build (including test) to detect integration errors as quickly as possible. Many teams find that this approach leads to significantly reduced integration problems and allows a team to develop cohesive software more rapidly.*

Kent Beck and Martin Fowler are credited as the first users of the term Continuous Integration since 1999. Now, more than 10 years later, this term has become a well-known and well-used practice (though many interested parties might wish it would turn into an established standard) used for software design and engineering across the entire industry.

The main essence of it lies in the simple practice of each delivering person in the team to meet on a very frequent, several-times-per-day basis to a source control repository.

In the long run, this could save us from lots of headaches and last-minute integrations made in a rush. The more frequent this integration is, the less chance you have to get an incompatible bunch of modules instead of a rock solid application.

Okay, so now you are delivering to a repository every so often but what next? Repository integration will keep the code consistent, but will it check the code for correctness or run some tests? The answer here is no. What we need at this time is some build automation, and here TeamCity steps in.

Features

Let's sum up some outstanding TeamCity features.

Automatic and manual build triggering

Do you want every change in the **Version Control System (VCS)** to be verified? It's never been easier. Just set up automatic build triggering on every commit and you are done. Also dependent builds could be instantly triggered after the completion of some other build and may even use their generated artifacts. At any time, we can schedule a manual build by simply clicking on the **Run** button.

Pre-tested commit

This concept also has another name—remote run. It is really a life saver when we wish to check the consistency of our patch with the whole project. Instead of performing a commit, we select **Remote run** on the commit screen and can decide whether to do an actual commit depending on build results. It is usually not a good idea to proceed with a commit if the build is either failed or did not introduce new failures itself, but kept previous ones in place.

Instant notifications

There are plenty of different ways to stay in touch with the TeamCity Server. On the other hand, it could be as simple as sending an e-mail to all interested parties and as exquisite as the Windows tray notifier. Many other options such as RSS feeds, Jabber, and plugins for major IDEs are supported.

Code coverage and inspections

Upon producing build results we may be interested in checking our code coverage. Further on, it is possible to apply over 600 IntelliJ IDEA's inspections in order to find actual and potential problems. Inspections result in thorough reports for probable bugs, performance issues, and obsolete code, if present.

Easy to verify code changes

No longer does the developer need to remember what the code looked like before a change had been introduced. TeamCity provides a very useful and effective comparison engine to easily see what actually has been modified with which changes.

Configurable test reports

You need not to wait for a long build run just to figure out that the very first test has failed. TeamCity will notify you at once when it notices a failing build. You will get a complete report showing which tests have failed, whether this problem has happened for the first time, and so on, with the full statistics the developer needs.

Comprehensive build infrastructure

TeamCity supports multiple multi-platform build agents which can be run in parallel independently of each other. It is possible to get workload information and history. Every bit of statistics related to builds is also accessible over time. It is possible to track build progress, run build chains, and apply enhanced build dependencies.

Enhanced VCS integration

TeamCity permits utilizing sophisticated VCS configuration. It can use a smart scheduling mechanism called **quiet period**, if there is a need not to run builds at once, but to wait until partial commits or ones from different roots are conducted. Agent-side checkout allows maintaining source code consistency over your builds spread between different build agents.

Advanced features

TeamCity provides flexible user management with the possibility of configuring per-project user roles and accesses along with user action audits. TeamCity supports adaptable user authentication with LDAP and NT authentication support, detection of hanging builds that take longer time than expected, discovery of JVM out-of-memory crashes, and on the fly thread dumps for running builds.

Terms and concepts

Let's look at some useful concepts that will help you understand TeamCity better.

Build agent

A build agent is an isolated software unit where actual builds are executed and run. A build agent can coexist with the TeamCity server on one physical box, however that is not required. It is possible to install two or more build agents on one machine though it is not the preferred way to go because of the performance impact those agents would have on each other:

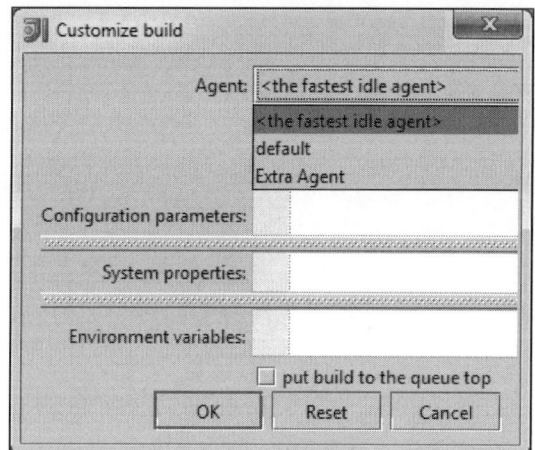

Sometimes separate build agents are needed per platform. For instance, it is often a situation that the server and the default agent are running on a Linux machine. Let's say there's a need to run some very specific kind of test such as GWT or flexunit tests on a build agent but this is impossible on a default one because these tests cannot be run in headless mode (it means display-less mode in which Linux servers usually work). A possible solution here is to install another build agent on the Windows machine. A build agent is a stateful machine. In order to make it work, the developer needs to install and run it first. At that point, the agent becomes disconnected. Then, during the configuration stage, we provide a connection link to the TeamCity server and the agent gets connected. It is still not yet ready because we need to make it authorized first. This is done manually on the **Agents** page. The default agent on the same machine as the server gets authorized automatically. At any point, you may disable or enable a particular build agent.

Build artifact

Every build may be configured to produce one or more build artifacts. They could be described as simple files that are possible to download or use in other (dependent) builds. For instance, the coverage data generated by a build is a build artifact. Also it could be some generated JAR, WAR, or other file that is configured.

There are also so-called hidden build artifacts that enlist raw coverage data and maven build data. These could be accessed through a special link.

Build configuration

In a nutshell, this is a set of actions to be applied to the source code. You define the actions and rules to be applied to the build, and click on **Run**; the configured builds would be handled by TeamCity and could be run from this point continuously and automatically. Creation of a build configuration is pretty straightforward and consists of several steps. On the first one, the name should be provided along with the rules describing how to understand if a build was successful or not. The later steps allow configuring version control settings, setting up build steps (Maven, Ant, and many other options are available). Then you can build triggering rules, dependencies, and other additional settings.

Upon creation of one build configuration, it could be replicated to avoid entering the configuration data many times in a row. Even a simple setting such as a user or group notification rule can be reused.

If you feel you are going to need the same build configuration several times, you may create a build configuration template. After that, you can generate new configurations with a single click—only the name of the template needs to be provided and the rest of the data would be served by the template.

Each build configuration has its state—active or paused. Also, it has a completion status that can be either successful, failed, or under investigation, indicated by the corresponding icon. Before the build has been run for the first time, there'll be no icon, as the status is still unknown.

Every build configuration has a unique ID, which you may refer to when performing some advanced manual configuration of TeamCity.

Code coverage

Code coverage is a very useful measure to describe the degree or level of how well and thoroughly the source code is covered by unit tests. This term really deserves a separate book to be written about it, though none are written yet. However, there are plenty of articles available on the Internet describing best practices. A nice start would be from the following example:

`http://en.wikipedia.org/wiki/Code_coverage`

There are many metrics that could be collected with powerful code coverage engines, TeamCity being one of them. Combined with the Sonar code inspection server (`sonarsource.org`) code coverage steps up to the next level where possible performance issues can be detected early on, probable bugs can be caught, or direct misuse of some language functions can be spotted.

TeamCity supports coverage engines for both Java and .NET. Major build runners that support code coverage collection include Maven, Ant, NAnt, NUnit, and several more.

At the time of writing, TeamCity did not support full coverage for integration tests. For example, having several Maven modules and calling one module from another will collect coverage for only the initiator module. In order to obtain this kind of coverage, the Sonar server with the Cobertura analysis tool would be needed.

My Changes

My changes is a special page where personal historical build information concerning a specific user is collected. Here, a user may observe his own changes and figure out how they affected builds presented by a timeline. You may go as far as viewing atomic change details presented by each build. Also the developer may navigate from here to the issue tracker directly, if issue tracker integration is turned on and properly configured.

Notifiers

TeamCity can utilize several notifiers. There can be either separate or common notification rules created for each of the supported notifiers. The total list includes:

- Email notifier undoubtedly being the most commonly used one
- IDE notifier shows status in your favorite IDE
- Jabber notifier sends events through Jabber server, that is Google Talk
- System Tray notifier displays updates in the Windows system tray
- Atom/RSS feed notifier informs you via Atom/RSS feed

Settings are configured on the **My Settings & Tools** page in the **Watched Builds and Notifications** section.

Pre-tested commit (remote run)

This delayed commit is a very powerful feature which previously allowed TeamCity to stand out in the crowd. By now, it has been adopted by major competitors as it became very useful, and therefore, popular. In short, it allows a developer to make sure that his changes will compile without problems and pass all tests, not only on his box but on at least one isolated machine.

Project

A project is the largest separate TeamCity's concept used here. It is merely a group of build configurations. It should have its own name, some meaningful description and may be used to define some generic security settings for all included build configurations. You can assign separate permissions for users on a per-project basis.

Version Control System

A Version Control System (VCS) is a facility to store a project's source code files and all changes made to them over time. It is expected that the VCS will represent corresponding versions of code for any given time. These slices are called revisions and are usually identified by incrementing numbers. TeamCity supports plenty of version control systems such as ClearCase, CVS, Git, Mercurial, Perforce, StarTeam, Subversion, Team Foundation Server, SourceGear Vault, and Visual SourceSafe.

Architecture

TeamCity is represented by a very simple and scalable distributed build grid architecture. There is one server, which is the central unit to which a bunch of build agents are connected. One default build agent comes with TeamCity itself and is usually installed on the same box containing the server. Other build agents can be installed elsewhere on UNIX/Linux/Windows platforms.

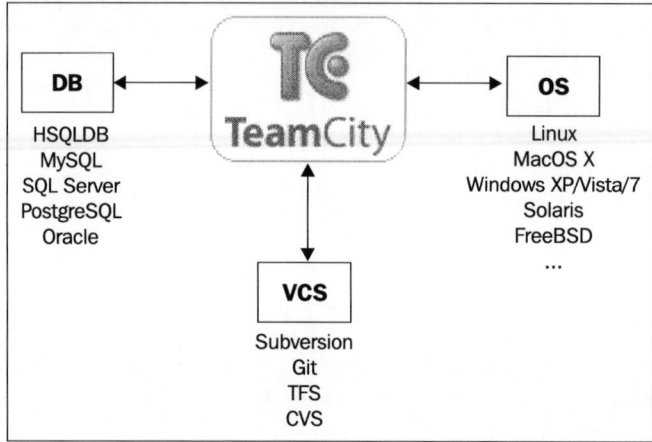

The server's duty is to coordinate cooperation of a build agent grid. Those are the facilities which actually run all the builds and tests—not the server. It runs nothing but a database where historical records are being stored, and a modest web application where they are shown. The server keeps a mediator role between agents, collecting and publishing all information data in one place.

Build lifecycle

The build lifecycle is depicted in the following diagram:

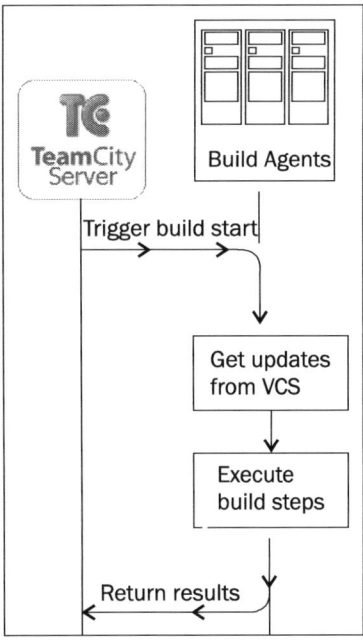

Scheduling to a build agent

The build process is always initiated by the TeamCity server. It could have a manual cause, that is after you've clicked on the **Run** button for a specific build. But more important for us is automatic triggering which could be originated from several independent origins. If you've set up VCS triggers, TeamCity can detect that a commit has been made to the version control system. Otherwise, it can discover that some build which we are depending on has finished successfully and then schedule our dependent build at once.

If there are no particular preferences for selecting a build agent that have been specified, TeamCity chooses the fastest idle one from its pool. But the build is not started yet—first it is being scheduled and put into the Build Queue, and when its turn comes later, it gets assigned to a particular agent and only then gets executed.

You need to pay attention to platform-specific builds and instruct your build agents to support only certain build configuration. Various agents could have different build paths or some environment settings, and so on, which could prevent your build from being successfully executed if it's picked up by the wrong agent.

VCS specifics

A build should be run on some source code and here's the place where powerful VCS integration steps in. The two feasible options for the build agent to be provided with needed sources to start the build are as follows:

- Server-side checkout
- Agent-side checkout

Server-side checkout

This is the default and most commonly used option. This way only the server cares about VCS configurations and support, thus freeing agents from any knowledge about how the VCS is used and how it is arranged. Among the pros, there are fewer and easier configurations on build agents, reduced interaction with the VCS altogether because the server manages all version control related operations. TeamCity sends only relevant incremental patches of the source files that it stores in its internal cache.

Agent-side checkout

Here the pros are that you are able to apply some version-specific actions, such as accessing the .svn directory for Subversion or retrieving the related revision numbers from the underlying VCS. Keep in mind that this option requires more effort to set up the configuration, and is not supported by every VCS available in TeamCity.

Running the build

When the source code is in place, the agent can start the build. Exact actions are described in so-called build-steps that were set up on the **Build Configuration** page. Each step can define its own specific goal, which is accomplished by the related build runner. A build runner could be thought of as a plugin for TeamCity supporting a particular build tool such as Ant, Maven, MSBuild, NAnt, test frameworks such as NUnit, or even the bare command line, and many others.

So you need to construct your build with several build steps. Running this build will execute all arranged steps in a defined sequence.

In real time, the build agent updates the server with the latest changes. All test reports and logged messages are being sent to TeamCity on the fly, so you are able to monitor the progress of the build in real time.

When the build is finished, its outcome will be sent to TeamCity, including coverage reports, built JAR and WAR files, together called **build artifacts**. Upon completion, you may download them from the server and investigate them if you wish.

Summary

TeamCity is a contemporary, rich-featured, distributed build management and Continuous Integration server. It has been designed for developers and by developers, thus being very intuitive, easy to use, easy to learn, and user friendly. There's absolutely nothing hard to understand neither in lifecycle, organization, or total workflow of TeamCity.

TeamCity contains an extensive set of utilities which moves your development effectiveness and comfort to a totally new level. It is a light and very easy to install facility which provides you with a decent degree of certainty that the code in your version control system not only compiles, but even adheres to written tests. And all this magic happens automatically on a continuous basis without requiring any user intervention. Every change in your source code would be detected, monitored and inspected, and you shall get full report about every modification introduced.

2
Sample Project

As we are now clear with the theory, let's get us some practice! In this chapter, we shall dive into writing actual code, starting from creating a development environment, followed by generating a sample project, and finally adding some unit tests to complete the picture.

Imagine a situation where there's a need to write an online calculation service available from anywhere around the world. Requirements ask for precise math and availability over the Internet. We'll start with creating a simple project which could benefit from introducing Continuous Integration.

In order to get a working environment for our sample project we shall need:

- **Java Development Kit (JDK)**: Major readers may already have one installed, anyway please check your version.
- **Maven**: Apache Maven is an impressively powerful and very popular software project management and comprehension tool. Full application lifecycle including creating, building, and running could be maintained by Maven and our project would be no exception.
- **IDE**: We shall use one from the creators of TeamCity—namely IntelliJ IDEA. The functionality provided by the free community edition should be perfectly enough for our needs. Eclipse users will not be left behind as support for their IDE is also fully provided by TeamCity, and will be described later in this book.

After all prerequisites are met, we will proceed with source generation using Maven, and then import the generated project into IntelliJ IDEA. That would be great time to create some business logic, write tests for it, and finally launch our application.

Creating the development environment

First things first, we need to verify that we have the proper JDK installed.

Installing JDK

For our project we shall use JDK 1.6, as TeamCity requires JRE 1.6 or newer versions.

It is unlikely that you don't have JDK on your computer. If you have everything ready, you can confirm that you're totally set up by running the following line in your command line prompt:

```
javac -version
```

You should see something like this:

```
javac 1.6.0_31
```

A similar output indicates that you are good to go with your system and can skip to the next section. The last two digits after the underscore represent the current update of your JDK. It does not really matter which exact minor version of JDK 1.6 you have.

If your actual output differs significantly, for example, showing some message complaining about a missing command, you need to install and set up your JDK.

First you need to go to `http://www.oracle.com/technetwork/java/javase/downloads/index.html` and scroll down to the most recent Java SE 6 update version and hit the **Download** button under the **JDK** column header. Make sure you are not downloading the JRE version because being a running environment (as its name says) it does not contain any development facilities such as javac compiler.

Then run the installation to the installation path you prefer; for example, `C:\Program Files\Java\jdk1.6.0_31\`.

Configuring your Windows environment

Now you need to get Java's installation directory into the system environment variable `JAVA_HOME`.

1. On the **Start** menu, right-click on **Computer**, then click on **Properties**, and choose **Advanced system settings** on the left pane. In the newly opened window, choose the **Advanced** tab and click on the **Environment Variables...** button:

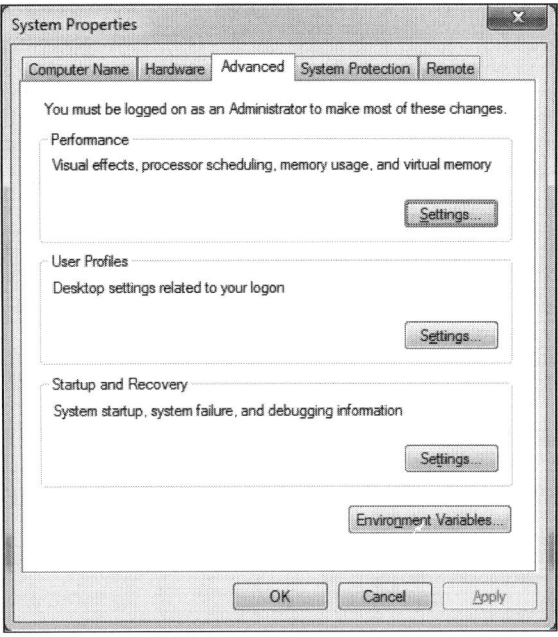

2. Check if you have **JAVA_HOME** already defined in **System variables** (the JDK installation process usually does that for you). If you don't have such a variable, click on the **New...** button and provide data similar to this:

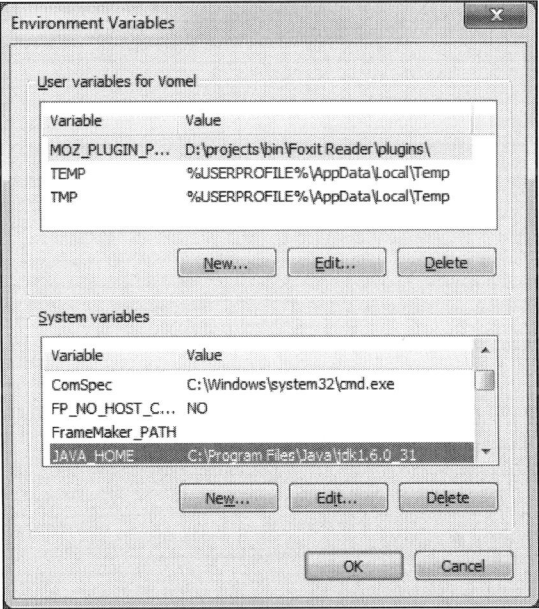

3. Then edit the Path variable by appending the %JAVA_HOME%\bin key to the current contents of the Path environment variable.

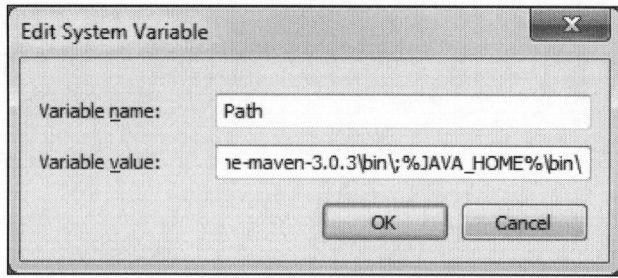

4. To verify that all is done, repeat the earlier command-line test and make sure your output looks like the expected one.

Installing Maven

At the time of writing this book, the latest Maven version is 3.0.4, so let's use that one. We will need Maven not for TeamCity server itself but for its build agent(s). Supported Maven versions are 2.x and 3.x so we are not constrained here and have plenty of available options to select from.

Maven could be downloaded from its Apache Project website: http://maven.apache.org/download.html. Pick the latest binary ZIP version and unpack it to some directory on your hard drive, say C:\workspace\maven. Having unpacked Maven you need to add its location into two system environment variables—MAVEN_HOME and M2_HOME—and then append the %MAVEN_HOME%\bin key to the Path environment variable.

In order to verify that Maven is ready—execute this line in your command line:

mvn -version

Then you should see something like the following line on your console:

Apache Maven 3.0.4

This indicates that we are all done here.

Creating a sample project

In order not to bother with writing boilerplate code, we can use the Apache Maven archetype plugin to create a skeleton for our future project.

Generating source by Maven

It is useful to keep one common directory for all your projects—it could be `C:\workspace`, for instance. Create it if you don't have it, and browse that folder via command line.

Copy-paste or manually enter the following command in one line (don't introduce line breaks—you see them here only because the width of the page does not allow fitting the whole command in one line):

```
C:\workspace>mvn archetype:generate -DgroupId=com.packtpub
  -DartifactId=sample -Dversion=1.0 -DarchetypeArtifactId=maven-
  archetype-webapp -DarchetypeGroupId=org.apache.maven.archetypes
  -DinteractiveMode=false
```

Here is some clarification for arguments shown in the previous command line:

- `archetype:generate`: It is a particular Maven goal and it instructs Maven to create projects based on some template
- `-DgroupId`: Usually you'll write your projects' common package here
- `-DartifactId`: The name of the project, pick whichever you like
- `-Dversion`: The current version of your project to synchronize dependencies
- `-DarchetypeArtifactId`: The name of the template for project creation
- `-DarchetypeGroupId`: The group for related and/or similar templates
- `-DinteractiveMode`: Turn off the confirmation dialog upon project generation

Maven will download all missing dependencies, generate the requested project, and should end its execution with a screen like this:

```
C:\Windows\system32\cmd.exe
[INFO] Generating project in Batch mode
[INFO] Archetype [org.apache.maven.archetypes:maven-archetype-webapp:1.0] found in
 catalog remote
[INFO] ------------------------------------------------------------------------
[INFO] Using following parameters for creating project from Old (1.x) Archetype: ma
ven-archetype-webapp:1.0
[INFO] ------------------------------------------------------------------------
[INFO] Parameter: groupId, Value: com.packtpub
[INFO] Parameter: packageName, Value: com.packtpub
[INFO] Parameter: package, Value: com.packtpub
[INFO] Parameter: artifactId, Value: sample
[INFO] Parameter: basedir, Value: c:\workspace
[INFO] Parameter: version, Value: 1.0
[INFO] project created from Old (1.x) Archetype in dir: c:\workspace\sample
[INFO] ------------------------------------------------------------------------
[INFO] BUILD SUCCESS
[INFO] ------------------------------------------------------------------------
[INFO] Total time: 5.572s
[INFO] Finished at: Mon Jun 04 03:05:03 EEST 2012
[INFO] Final Memory: 8M/114M
[INFO] ------------------------------------------------------------------------
c:\workspace>
```

You do not have to remember the exact wording of this command. It is possible to find reference to the Maven archetype plugin on the respective Apache project website: http://maven.apache.org/archetype/maven-archetype-plugin/ and discover its potentials.

Installing IntelliJ IDEA

Get the latest community edition of IntelliJ IDEA from http://www.jetbrains.com/idea/download/index.html and install it into the desired location on your hard drive. The installation is pretty straightforward and should not raise any questions.

Opening your project with IDEA

The steps for opening your project using IDEA are as follows:

1. Launch IDEA and click on the **Create New Project** button:

Chapter 2

2. Select **Import project from external model** and choose **Maven**:

3. Now select **Root directory** of the sample project previously generated by Maven. There are too many settings available on this page which may confuse a new user at this point. It is strongly recommended to check the **Import Maven projects automatically** and **Automatically download: Sources** checkboxes. The former option will force IDEA to do most of the Maven-related configurations for you on the fly, whereas the latter will automatically download sources of third-party libraries whenever available.

Sample Project

4. Other checkboxes could be selected as shown in the following screenshot:

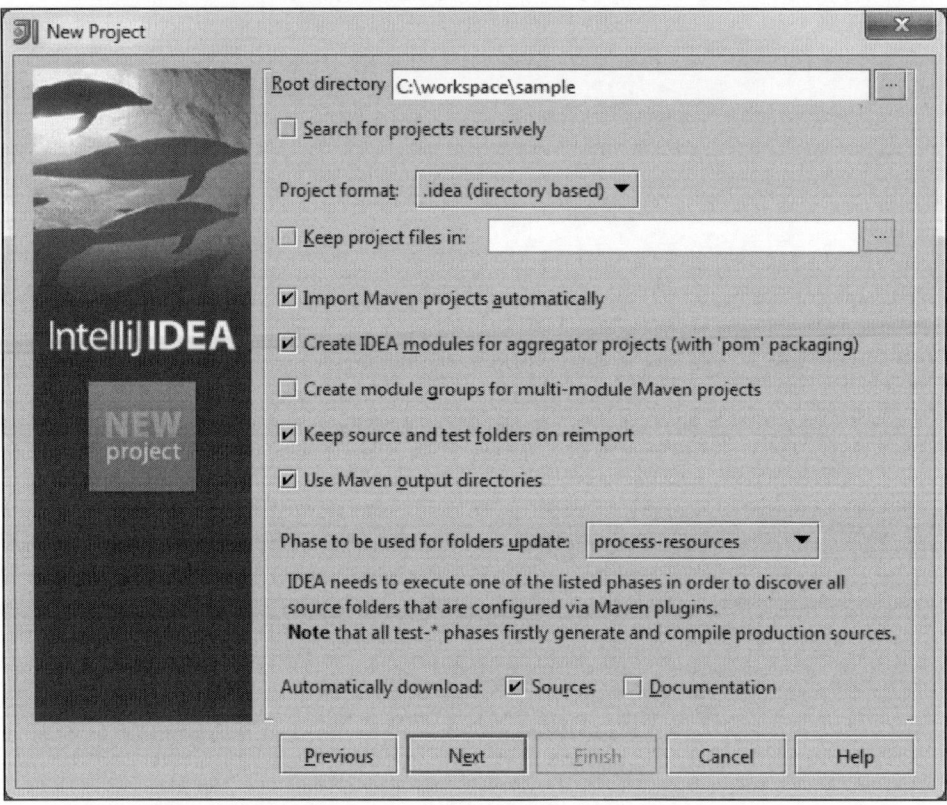

5. The following screen tells us that IDEA has detected a valid Maven project in the directory specified in the previous step:

6. Then we need to provide the location of Java SDK. Hit the plus button, select **JSDK**, and browse to the JDK installation directory (`C:\Program Files\Java\jdk1.6.0_31`).

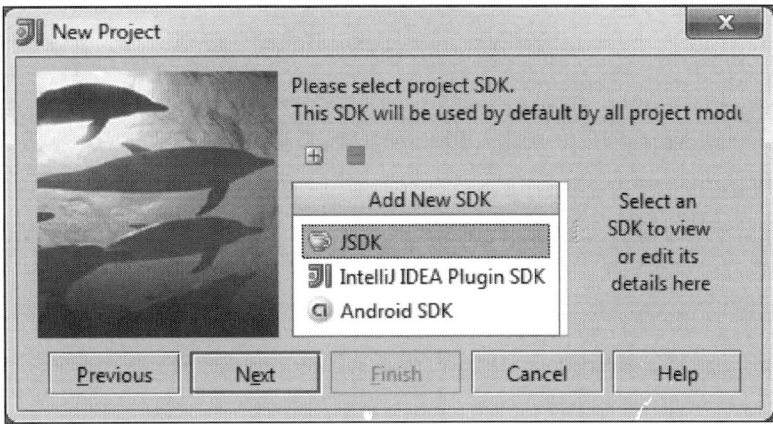

IDEA displays the detected JSDK version and its core libraries.

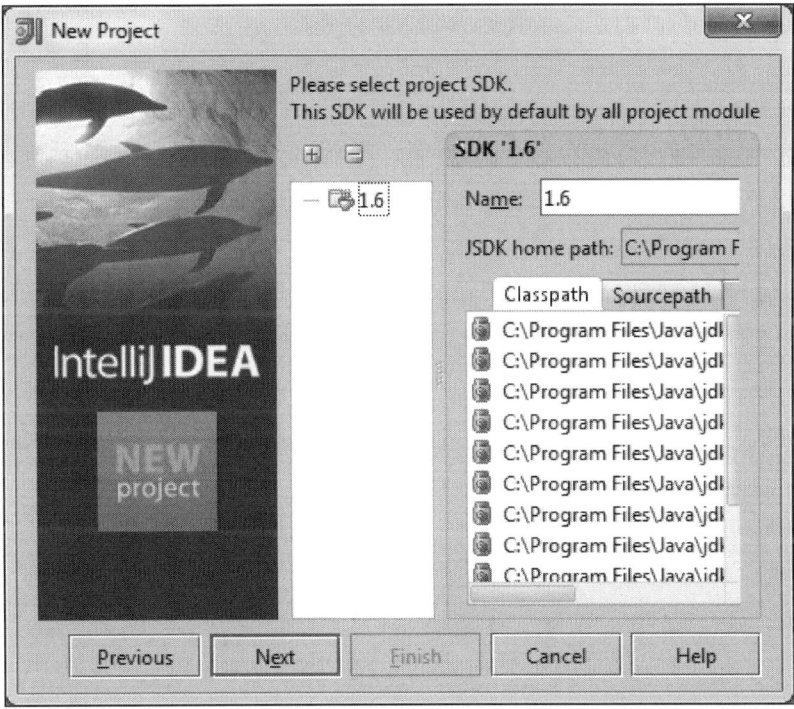

Sample Project

7. Confirm the project's name and click on **Finish**.

Phew! We're done here. Now IDEA opens our project and we can see the base directory structure that Maven archetype plugin has generated for us along with several required files we can start our development with.

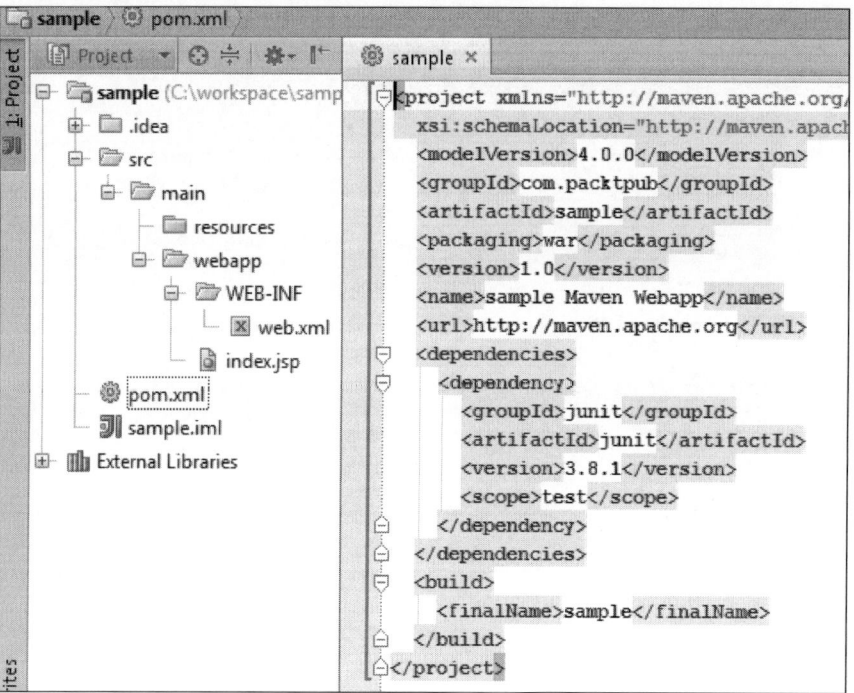

[28]

Adding unit tests

To start with, let's write a simple Java class and put it into a suitable package. After that we can write some tests to see if it works as expected.

Creating some testable code

First we need to create a Java file, which will contain our business logic. On the project browser screen, right-click on the **main** folder, choose **New** | **Directory**, and input `java` as the folder name. Then go to **File** | **Project Structure** and select **Modules** on the left. On the right, select the **Sources** tab, traverse to and right-click on the **java** folder and mark it as **Sources** with the respective blue folder icon.

Also, we shall need to test the destination package where they will reside. Similar to the previous method—right-click on the **src** folder, choose **New** | **Directory** | **test/ java**. Then, again visit the **Sources** tab at **File** | **Project Structure** | **Modules**, expand the **src** directory and find the new **test** folder with the nested **java** directory under it. This time when you right-click on **java** under the **test** folder, mark it as **Test Sources** by using the corresponding sign of the same name.

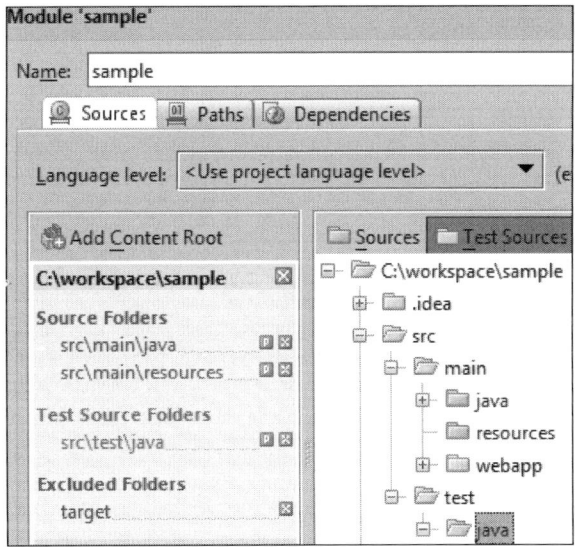

After this operation, IDEA comes to know that the **java** folder serves as a container for java source code and the **test** folder should contain related tests. Now right-click on the **java** directory again and select **New** | **Java Class**. Enter `com.packtpub. Calculator` there—it will act as the business logic center of our project.

Sample Project

The logic itself could be pretty simple for now and will look like this:

```
package com.packtpub;
public class Calculator {
    public int sum(int x, int y) {
        return x + y;
    }
}
```

> **Downloading the example code**
> You can download the example code files for all Packt books you have purchased from your account at http://www.PacktPub.com. If you purchased this book elsewhere, you can visit http://www.PacktPub.com/support and register to have the files e-mailed directly to you.

Writing your first test

At last, we have some testable logic here—so let's write our first test!

1. Having your cursor anywhere within the Calculator.java file press *Ctrl + Shift + T*, click on **Create New Test** and select the required options. Check the **sum** method and click on **OK**.

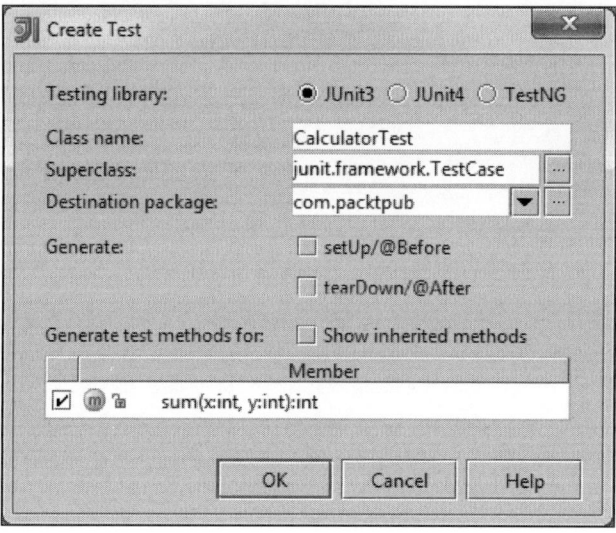

2. Choose the offered destination directory and click on **OK**.

Chapter 2

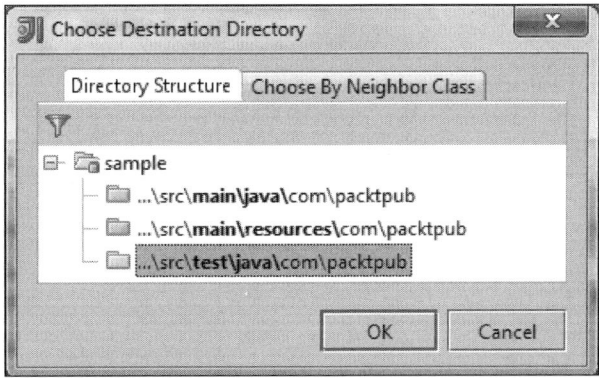

At this step, IDEA automatically generates the test stub with this content:

```
package com.packtpub;
import junit.framework.TestCase;
public class CalculatorTest extends TestCase {
    public void testSum() throws Exception {

    }
}
```

Let's implement the `testSum()` method:

```
public void testSum() throws Exception {
    Calculator calculator = new Calculator();
    int sum = calculator.sum(1, 2);
    Assert.assertEquals(3, sum);
}
```

3. Now we can run the test. Right-click on the `testSum` method and choose **Run 'testSum()'** in the pop-up window.

After the test completes successfully, IDEA will show a green **ok** circle with the text **All Tests Passed**.

Launching our application

After making sure that our business logic works as expected we may wish to finally run our application. In order to achieve this, we need to introduce some last configuration changes into our `pom.xml` file. We shall use the `jetty` HTTP server and servlet container. Now what is needed to be done is these lines have to be added into `pom.xml` within the `<build>` tag as follows:

```
<build>
    <finalName>sample</finalName>
    <plugins>
        <plugin>
            <groupId>org.mortbay.jetty</groupId>
            <artifactId>maven-jetty-plugin</artifactId>
            <version>6.1.10</version>
        </plugin>
    </plugins>
</build>
```

Also let's update the `index.jsp` file to make use of our calculator:

```
<%@ page import="com.packtpub.Calculator" %><%
    Calculator calculator = new Calculator();
    int sum = calculator.sum(1, 2);
    out.print("1 + 2 = " + sum);
%>
```

Now we need to launch the jetty server. The easiest way to do this is through the corresponding Maven goal which is called `jetty:run`. Select **Run | Edit Configurations... | + | Maven**, provide the name (that is, `jetty:run`), then choose the home of the project as working directory and enter `jetty:run` in the **Goals** text input. Check the **Make** checkbox in order to compile the project every time before each launch of this configuration, and click on **OK**.

Now, in the **Run Configurations** drop-down box, you'll see a new element with the name you've provided in the previous step (say, **jetty:run**). Choose this configuration and select **Run | Run 'jetty:run'** on the menu.

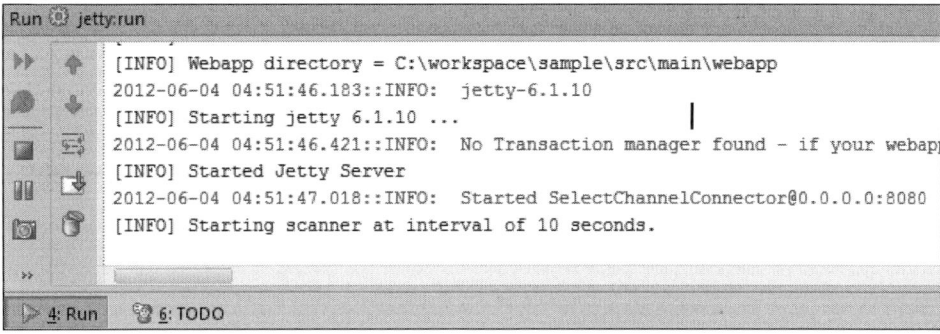

As you can see from the output, the jetty server has been started on your machine on port 8080. Now visit http://localhost:8080/sample with your browser and see what happens.

Voila, we've made it!

Summary

In this chapter we've prepared our development environment, and installed all the required facilities such as JDK, Maven, and IDE to start from.

Henceforth we will have a working web application based on the template generated by the Maven archetype plugin. In the application, we have configured a separate business logic package with classes providing services to the web page. We also have a specific package containing a test against our business logic.

In the next chapter, we shall be preparing our Continuous Integration environment. We will install the TeamCity server with the included default build agent and run them.

3
Preparing a Continuous Integration Environment

This chapter will provide a brief glimpse into TeamCity's internal working. In order to have a minimum working TeamCity suite, the user requires a TeamCity server and at least one build agent. TeamCity can be downloaded from http://www.jetbrains.com/teamcity/download/index.html. The downloaded TeamCity bundle contains a server for a particular platform and a bunch of build agents for all supported platforms. Currently TeamCity can be installed onto Windows, Mac OS X, and Linux operating systems.

No more downloads are required after that. Plugins for supported IDEs are already included in the bundle and can be later installed on demand.

Hardware requirements

TeamCity server and build agents serve different purposes. Thus, requirements for them are also different.

Build agent

Its system requirements depend on the actual builds that are expected to be run on it, so hardware configuration should be chosen accordingly. For example, if you use a Maven build on your machine and it works fine, it means that the current configuration would be sufficient since it has been complemented with about 500 MB for the agent itself. Please be aware that running several agents on a single machine is possible but not recommended as they will fight for available resources, degrading the total performance of each other.

Server

The server acts as a general collector and presenter of all data generated by builds on connected build agents. Therefore, its performance relies heavily on the number of simultaneously connected agents, the number of open web application pages, and the IDE plugin that the user is logged in to. Also, the traffic that is generated while communicating with clients described previously could yield a major bottleneck. This could happen if, for example, the generated logs in build configurations are very verbose and there are many build configurations activated at once. Also, the quantity of VCSs and the frequency of their status checks could play a significant role in the overall server operation.

Jetbrains publishes the following information describing a reliable setup on their wiki: `http://confluence.jetbrains.net/display/TCD7/How+To...#HowTo...-EstimatehardwarerequirementsforTeamCity`.

> Based on our experience, a modest hardware such as a 3.2 dual core CPU, with a 3.2 GB memory under Windows, and a 1 GB network adapter can provide acceptable performance for the following setup:
> - 60 projects and 300 build configurations (one fourth being run regularly)
> - More than 300 builds a day
> - About 2 MB log per build
> - 50 build agents
> - 50 web users and 30 IDE users
> - 100 VCS roots (mainly Perforce and Subversion using server checkout), average interval for checking changes is 120 seconds
> - More than 150 changes per day
>
> The database (`MySQL`) is running on the same machine, the main TeamCity process has `-Xmx1100m -XX:MaxPermSize=120m` JVM settings.
>
> However, to ensure peak load can be handled well, more powerful hardware is recommended.

Based on the author's experience, for small teams/projects it is usually enough to have a single core 1.7 GHz CPU, 1 GB RAM, and 20 GB of HDD space for the server and one build agent installed on the same machine.

Installing TeamCity server

Great news is that the professional version comes for free. It's fully functional without any crucial shortcomings. What makes professional different from the paid enterprise version is the number of concurrently supported build configurations and the number of build agents connected at once. That limit is moderate and usually should not be exceeded to ensure comfortable development with all the advantages of Continuous Integration.

At the time of writing, the free version permits three coexisting build agents and 20 simultaneous build configurations. Each extra agent will be charged separately. It is always possible to buy an enterprise license for $1999 (at the time of writing) and get rid of all restrictions.

If you already have a running TeamCity bundle and are willing to upgrade it to the latest version, please refer to *Chapter 7, Advanced Configuration* of this book.

There are three packages available for download:

- The *.exe installation file effective for Windows only
- The *.tar.gz distribution bundle for all platforms (including Windows)
- The *.war (web application archive) package that could be deployed into an existing J2EE web servlet container such as Tomcat 7

Installing the Windows distribution

This is apparently the most verbose installation option of all three, as during the installation process the user is shown almost every available configuration setting with a possibility to alter it right away.

1. Accept the license agreement, choose an appropriate destination folder (in this book we will use the `D:\TeamCity` installation path), and select the desired components for installation.

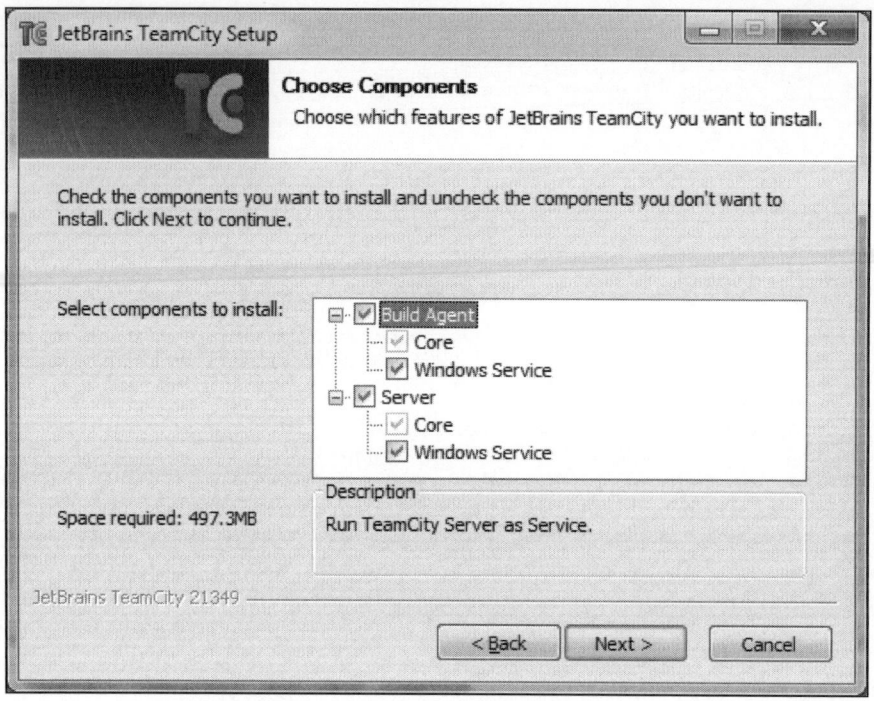

2. As shown in the previous screenshot, **Build Agent** can be installed along with **Server**.

> It is preferable to use the **Windows Service** option as it offers easier maintenance. These services could be then managed by standard Windows services application (right-click on **Computer** and select **Manage** | **Services** and **Applications** | **Services**).
>
> There are certain occasions when there's no administrative access to target computer so we have to abandon the **Windows Service** option and use regular scripts included for startup/shutdown.

3. At that time, you need to select an appropriate destination directory where the configuration files will reside and finally, select a port on which the TeamCity server will be listening.

   Please keep in mind that you may already have some other software using this port on your machine (such as IIS or something else). You can check for currently used ports via the following command on Windows (requires administrator privileges):

   `C:\netstat -abn > stat.txt`

   Upon completion, check the generated `C:\stat.txt` file for the line with port `80`.

   `TCP     0.0.0.0:80     0.0.0.0:0        LISTENING [some_program_name.exe]`

   If you can find such line it means that the mentioned port is occupied and in the last column you should see the name of the application that is in charge of it. You may either disable this application or choose another port to use, such as `8111`, for instance.

   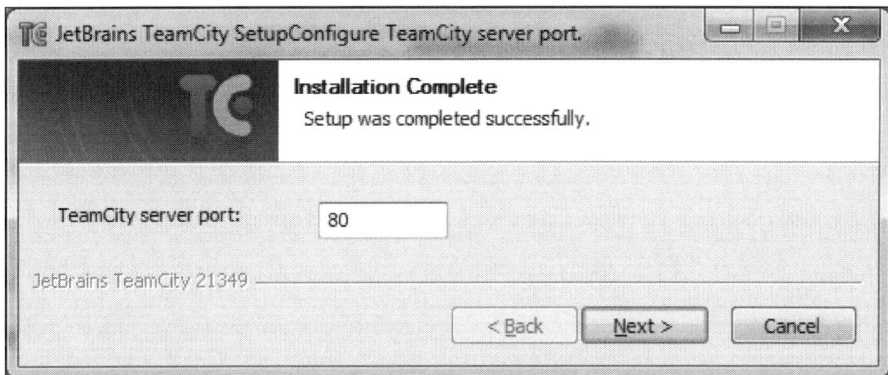

4. The initial TeamCity server configuration is now complete.

Installing the Linux multi-platform distribution

The TeamCity universal multi-platform suite can be installed on major popular operating systems including Windows, Mac OS X, and Linux.

Let's go through an example installation on a Linux machine. First you need to download an application archive. You may either use a link from the TeamCity website or a plain command line if you know the exact version you want (the next command should be written in a single line):

`[root@host]# wget http://download-ln.jetbrains.com/teamcity/TeamCity-7.0.2.tar.gz`

```
[root@ host]# wget http://download-ln.jetbrains.com/teamcity/TeamCity-7.0.2.tar.gz
--2012-10-31 15:56:22--  http://download-ln.jetbrains.com/teamcity/TeamCity-7.0.2.tar.gz
Resolving download-ln.jetbrains.com... 87.248.201.121, 87.248.202.148
Connecting to download-ln.jetbrains.com|87.248.201.121|:80... connected.
HTTP request sent, awaiting response... 200 OK
Length: 381775816 (364M) [application/x-tar-gz]
Saving to: TeamCity-7.0.2.tar.gz

100%[=====================================================>] 381,775,816 1.65M/s   in 3m 46s

2012-10-31 16:00:09 (1.61 MB/s) - TeamCity-7.0.2.tar.gz
[root@ host]#
```

You need to unpack the downloaded `*.tar.gz` archive into the desired directory. Please make sure that the `JAVA_HOME` system environment variable is defined and valid, otherwise the TeamCity server will fail to start.

All maintenance is done with corresponding shell scripts made available for all supported platforms. Scripts are located in the `/bin` directory of the TeamCity installation.

To start and stop the server and the default build agent, use the following commands respectively:

- `runAll.sh start`
- `runAll.sh stop`

The corresponding script file for Windows distribution is called `runAll.bat` and its syntax is the same as mentioned previously.

```
[root@host]# ./runAll.sh start
Using CATALINA_BASE:   /opt/TeamCity
Using CATALINA_HOME:   /opt/TeamCity
Using CATALINA_TMPDIR: /opt/TeamCity/temp
Using JRE_HOME:        /usr/java/jdk1.6u31/jre
Using CLASSPATH:       /opt/TeamCity/bin/bootstrap.jar:/opt/TeamCity/bin/tomcat-juli.jar
Starting TeamCity build agent...
Java executable is found in '/usr/java/jdk1.6u31/jre'.
Starting TeamCity Build Agent Launcher...
Agent home directory is /opt/TeamCity/buildAgent
Current Java runtime version is 1.6
Lock file: /opt/TeamCity/buildAgent/logs/buildAgent.properties.lock
Using no lock
Done [8348], see log at ../logs/teamcity-agent.log
[root@host]#
```

Multi-platform distribution on Linux, by default, tries to use port 8111 which is okay. Here we will use 192.168.1.1 as an IP address of the Linux machine on which we're installing TeamCity. If we browse the link **192.168.1.1:8111/maintenance/first.html** now, we shall see the following greeting page:

As it can be seen, TeamCity informs you that the home directory of the current user will be used by default. To override this setting, you need to point the TEAMCITY_DATA_PATH environment variable to the desired directory and restart TeamCity. After clicking on **Proceed,** you shall see a message that the TeamCity server is starting up, and in a matter of minutes, a **License Agreement** page will appear where you must accept the printed agreement, and click on **Continue**. All further steps are similar to the ones from the *Running the TeamCity server* section.

Installing from the WAR archive

Ensure that Sun/Oracle JRE with Version 1.6 or higher is present. Please be warned that OpenJDK is not supported.

You would also need J2EE Platform 1.4 or newer version of web container with Servlet API version 2.4 and newer.

 Jetbrains itself recommends to use Tomcat 6.0.27 or newer versions as all the previous versions could have some issues with TeamCity. And the best way to go is Tomcat 7, as it is free from major bugs existing in previous versions, and should not have issues with the TeamCity server.

Rename the `TeamCity-X.Y.Z.war` file to `TeamCity.war` to avoid version numbers from getting into the URL of the respective web application. Copy the obtained archive with truncated version into the deployment directory of your web application server.

In order to deploy TeamCity to the Tomcat container, you need to update Tomcat's /conf/server.xml file. Add the `useBodyEncodingForURI="true"` attribute to the `Connector` tag. If deploying is done into Jetty 7.0.2 or a higher version, it is necessary to configure the web application container in order to unpack the deployed WAR files.

If the web application server does not conduct automatic deployment of the web application, you should either manually deploy it via web server administration interface, or by simply restarting the server.

Installing the build agent

For the TeamCity suite to function properly, we need at least one build agent to be installed, connected, and authorized on the server.

Installing a default build agent

The multi-platform distribution (on Linux, for example) will install a default build agent automatically.

If you are installing the Windows *.exe package, then right after completing the server installation, it's time to provide configuration information for the default build agent. At this point, you are going to be presented with a configuration screen where you can edit the agent's default settings straightaway.

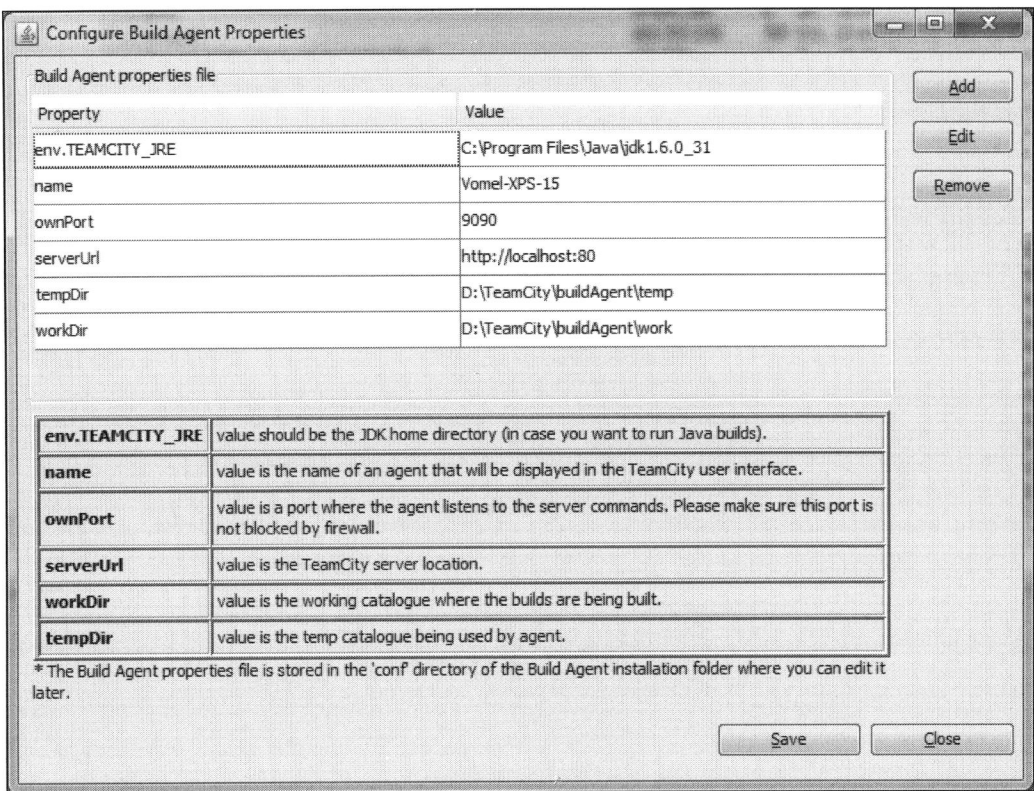

Every editable property is very well described in the bottom pane of the previous window. Upon submitting, you'll get a confirmation tip telling you where to look for the saved configuration in order to review or change it.

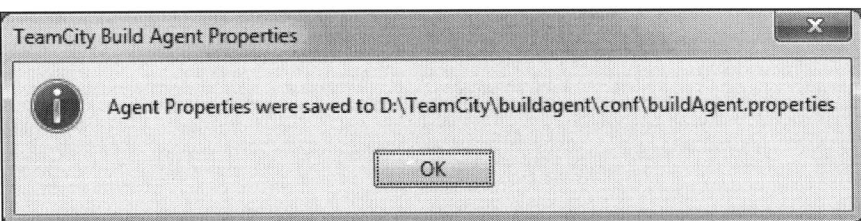

Remember this path for possible later updates, if required. After that, you need to choose whether the agent service would be run either under SYSTEM or a user account. Here, either preference is suitable. The only difference is that running under the SYSTEM account requires administrative rights, and could not be available as an option. Running a service under a user account imposes some requirements as well. An important one could be that the requested user should have write permissions in the TeamCity data directory.

The next screen asks whether you wish to start a build agent and/or TeamCity server right now.

This is the last step of the Windows bundle installation and finally, it is possible to opt for the automatic opening of the TeamCity server welcome page upon setup completion.

Running the TeamCity server

As we are now done with the installation procedures, let's see the result of our actions:

1. Browse to `http://localhost` and you will see something like this:

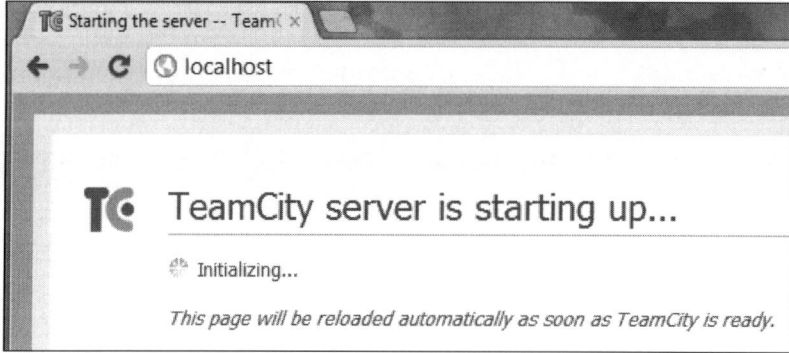

Chapter 3

2. After some time, the server fully initializes, the page is refreshed, and at this time, it offers us the option to create an administrator account.

3. Provide the required **Username** and **Password** values, and click on **Create Account**. You will be presented with the TeamCity welcome screen.

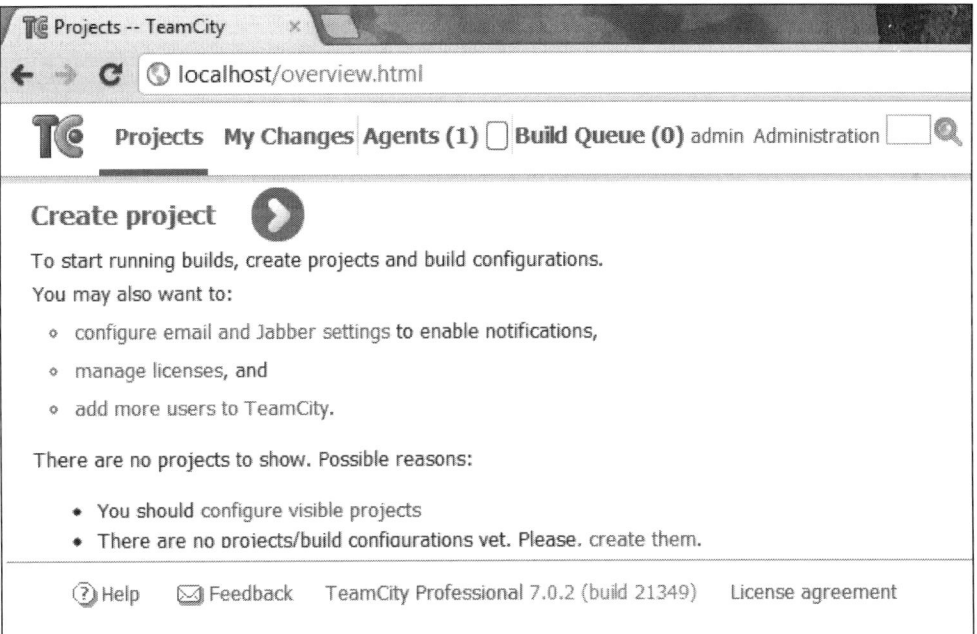

[45]

The selected (underlined by a thick blue bar) **Projects** tab shows that there are no projects created yet and you are welcome to create the first one. The next tab is **My Changes** which aggregates all the workflow data related to the current user. Then there's the **Agents** tab which shows the number of connected and authorized build agents in parentheses (currently showing **1** for the default agent configured recently). The white square to the right changes its color to dark blue when that single agent is busy. If there are multiple agents in use, the square will be divided into equal sections in proportion to the number of agents, and those sections will highlight their respective agents' statuses.

Following it is the **Build Queue** tab, which provides control over queued builds and allows rearranging their order, or ultimately deleting selected ones. The figure in parentheses shows the actual number of builds that are currently in the queue.

Next is the **admin** link, named after the current user's username, leading to a personal profile settings sheet and an **Administration** section, which combines all administrative activities and is only visible to users with admin rights.

The last control in the page header is a search box, which is of no use at this time as there are no build configurations created yet. Searching in TeamCity is a significant topic of its own. All relevant information that is being collected during builds can be later found via search. TeamCity utilizes Lucene query syntax. For example:

```
project:abc AND status:failed
```

This query will yield all failed builds for a project with name `abc`. The search tool supports `*` and `?` wildcards, or you may look for particular build numbers with `#<number>` statement. In order to find more detailed material on available search keywords and other related information for TeamCity, you can visit the `http://confluence.jetbrains.net/display/TCD7/Search` documentation page.

Summary

In this chapter, we've installed the TeamCity server and build agent bundle accommodated for our platform demands. Also some initial configuration has been provided for both, server and default agent.

We've managed to launch the TeamCity server, create the main administrative account, and browse the server's welcome page. Now we have a TeamCity server that is installed and ready to be configured for running our sample project's build in the next chapter.

4
Configuring the TeamCity Server

It is now time to see TeamCity in full power. This chapter shows how to connect a TeamCity server to a previously created sample project. We shall create a TeamCity project and its associated build configuration. The next step would be to force the build to be triggered automatically rather than manually. Then we'll go through some administration settings, add new users to the TeamCity, set up new customized e-mail notification rules, and learn about other notification options.

In this chapter you'll know how to:

- Add a new project to the version control system
- Create a project build configuration on TeamCity
- Set up automatic build triggering
- Configure and maintain users and their permissions
- Arrange useful build status notifications

Prerequisites

For the TeamCity server to be able to run certain code, this code needs to be placed in some version control system first. If you already have an existing project somewhere under version control, you may skip this paragraph altogether. Otherwise bear with me for a while and let's commit our sample project into the Subversion server.

> Setting up the SVN server is beyond this book's scope but you may download, install, and play around with a ton of free available choices. For example, you can try a pretty simple and straightforward Visual SVN server for Windows from http://www.visualsvn.com/server.

Configuring the TeamCity Server

In order to do a commit, you can perform the following steps:

1. In IntelliJ IDEA go to **VCS | Enable Version Control Integration** and select one of the registered VCSs that is used in your project—Subversion, for example (for other providers the exact actions may differ slightly but the main idea stays the same).

2. Then right-click on the project's name and select **Subversion | Share Directory...**.

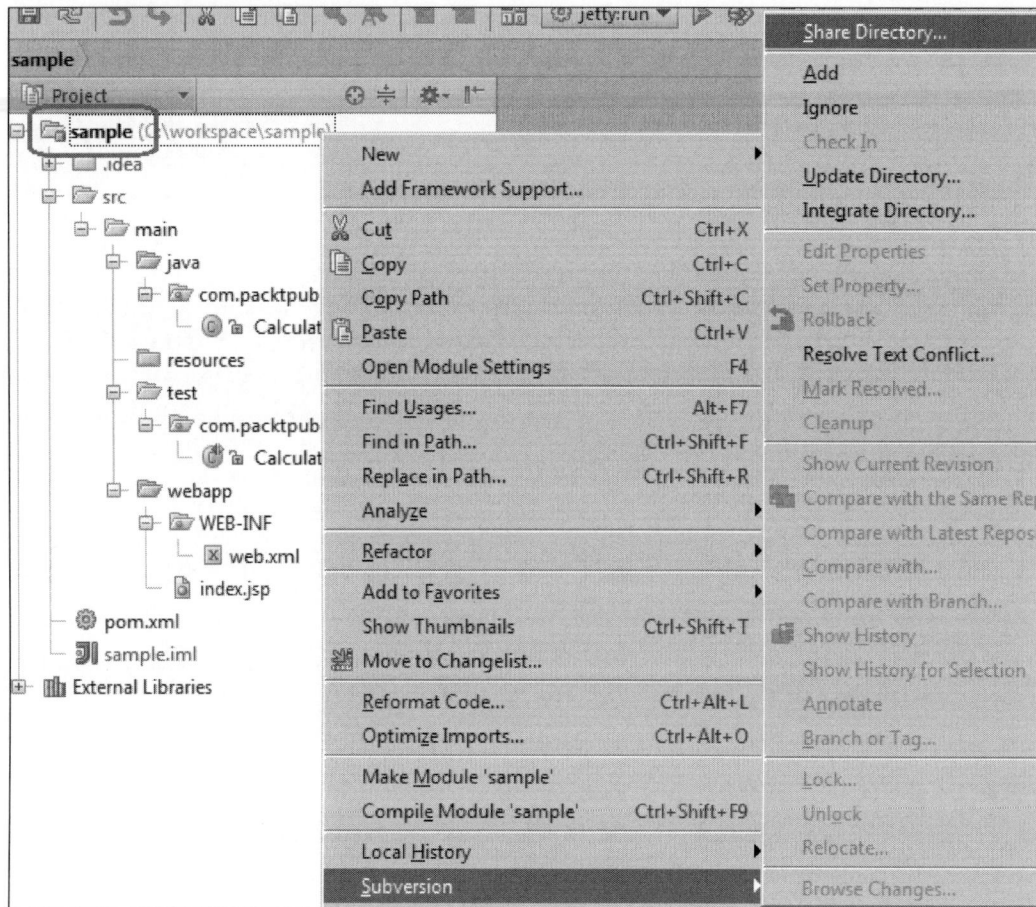

3. Click on the plus symbol, enter your Subversion server's URL, and click on **Share**.

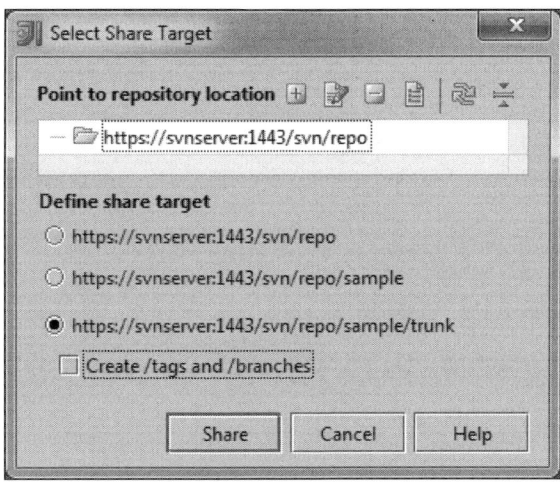

4. After this sharing step, you need to commit your project to Subversion. Select the `src` directory together with the `pom.xml` file, right-click on one of them and then go to **Subversion | Commit Files**. Enter some valid comment and click on **Commit**. Now we have some source to apply Continuous Integration to.

Working with projects and build configurations

In order to let our source be served by TeamCity, we need to have a project and build configuration arranged properly.

Creating a project

It's now time to create our first project in TeamCity and set up an appropriate build configuration for it. Visit `http://localhost/overview.html` — the page we left at the end of the previous chapter, and click on the **Create Project** link with the big right arrow icon.

At the first step we need to provide an appropriate name, which is a required property as noted by a red asterisk. Upon submitting, you should get a confirmation screen offering to create new a build configuration.

> Project "Sample" has been successfully created.
> Please add a build configuration for this project.

Creating a build configuration

Creation of a build configuration is done via a multi-step setup wizard that guides you through the whole process. It is not an irreversible procedure, so every setting could be revised and changed anytime later.

As usual, we must provide a relevant name first. Enter a relevant name (say, Unit Tests) and click on the **VCS Settings** button to proceed to the next step.

The **Version Control Settings** page would display a message saying that there are no VCS roots attached to this build configuration yet, so it is needed to create one. Click on the **Create and attach new VCS root** button to do it. Choose **Type of VCS** as **Subversion**, provide **VCS root name** to later distinguish it among the possible others. If you omit this property, the name will be generated automatically based on the next required property **URL**.

Provide the **URL**, **User name**, **Password**, and one more important property here—the applicable **Working Copy Format** option.

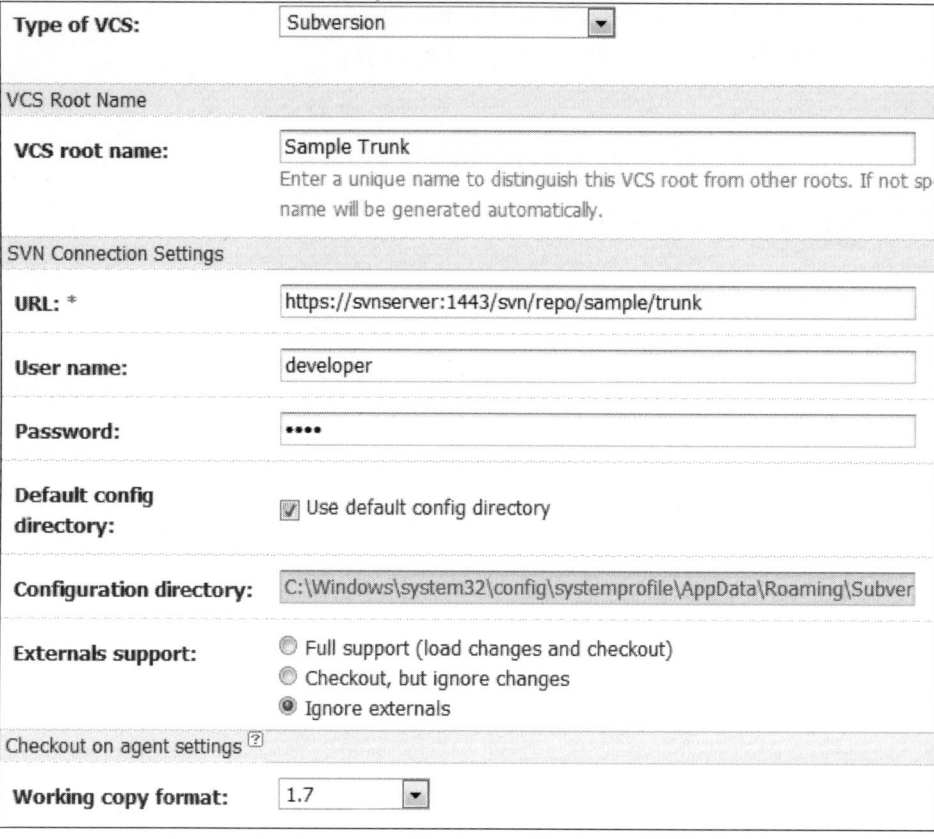

You may also wish to make this VCS root available to all projects with a related checkbox. After providing all the data, it is possible to test the connection right away with a dedicated button. This should give you a small confirmation message box saying that the connection is successful. Now click on the **Save** button to finish the VCS root setup. This action will bring you back to the former **Create Build Configuration** screen, which earlier said it doesn't have configured VCS roots. Now it states that we have a dedicated VCS root attached to the build configuration.

At this point, the tiresome part is done and it's now time for the interesting part. Click on **Add Build Step**. Here you need to select an appropriate build runner type. We're using Maven, so select it. The page will refresh and you'll be presented with many options, but having all Maven and Java settings (introduced in *Chapter 2, Sample Project*) in place, we would only need to provide **Goals**. Enter the **clean compile install** goals there.

It asks Maven respectively to clean existing compiled code, then compile the latest sources, run tests, and finally package our project into a Java archive and place it into Maven's local repository. All other settings can be left with their default values.

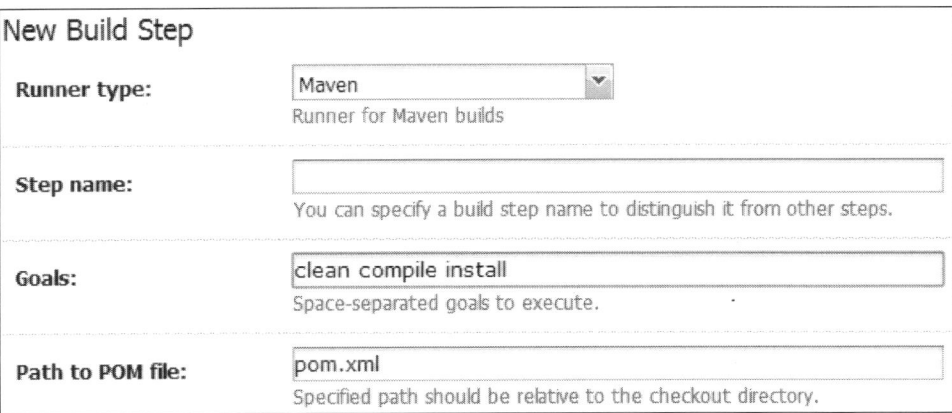

Now click on **Save** to complete the wizard. You should get a confirmation that the build configuration unit tests have been created successfully. At the moment, all the initially required steps are done and we have more than enough settings for an immediate run.

Configuring the TeamCity Server

If we now go to the main overview page, we'll see our freshly created **Sample** project and its sole **Unit Tests** build configuration.

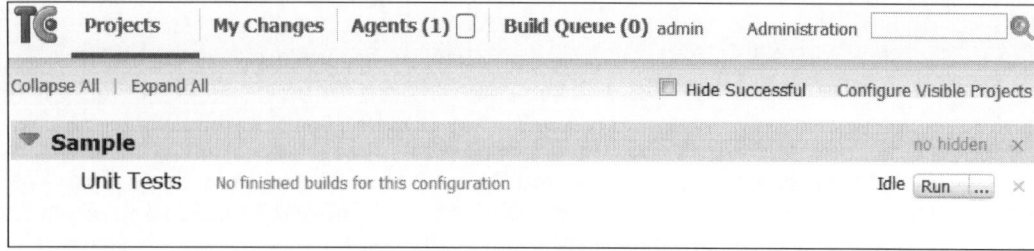

Running the build configuration

What we can do now is run our build by simply clicking on the **Run** button at the top-right corner and observe the very first build starting.

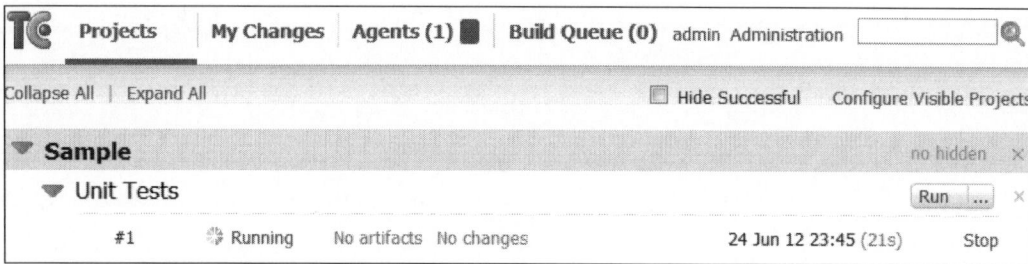

This very first build can take an unexpectedly long time to complete because it needs to download all the necessary Maven dependencies from the global repository and place them in a local one (provided at the Maven configuration step).

Now while this build is running (or right after it has succeeded), let's introduce a small change in the project's source code. Add a new line into `CalculatorTest.java` and perform a commit into Subversion. Upon checking the overview page of TeamCity, there are two interesting notes for us to make.

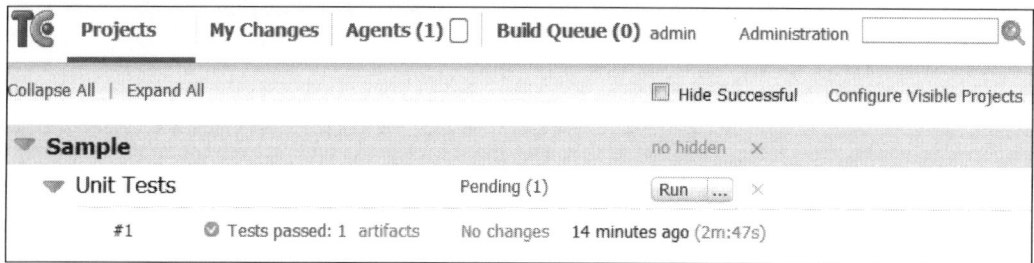

One is the successful status of our build's single test, and another one is a notion of the fact that TeamCity has detected a recent change in the source code and put the related **Pending (1)** link to the right of the build configuration's name.

After several commit-and-run cycles the start page of TeamCity will look something like this:

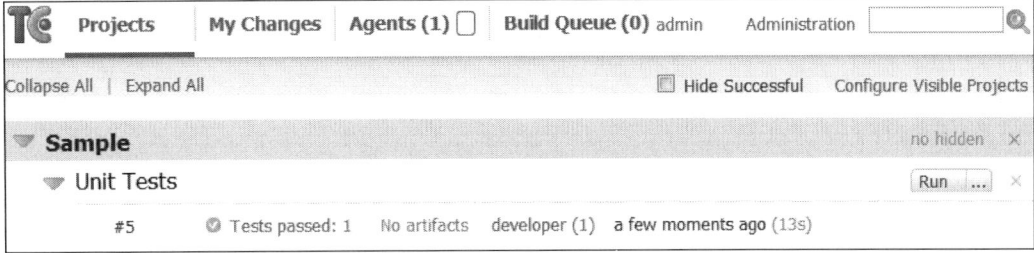

Triggering builds automatically

We will now see how to force TeamCity to run a build automatically upon detecting a change. It is worth remembering that all this is about Continuous Integration.

When you click on the build configuration's name (**Unit Tests**) you are presented with an overview page for this configuration. Here you can see the history of recent builds with a brief description of each of them.

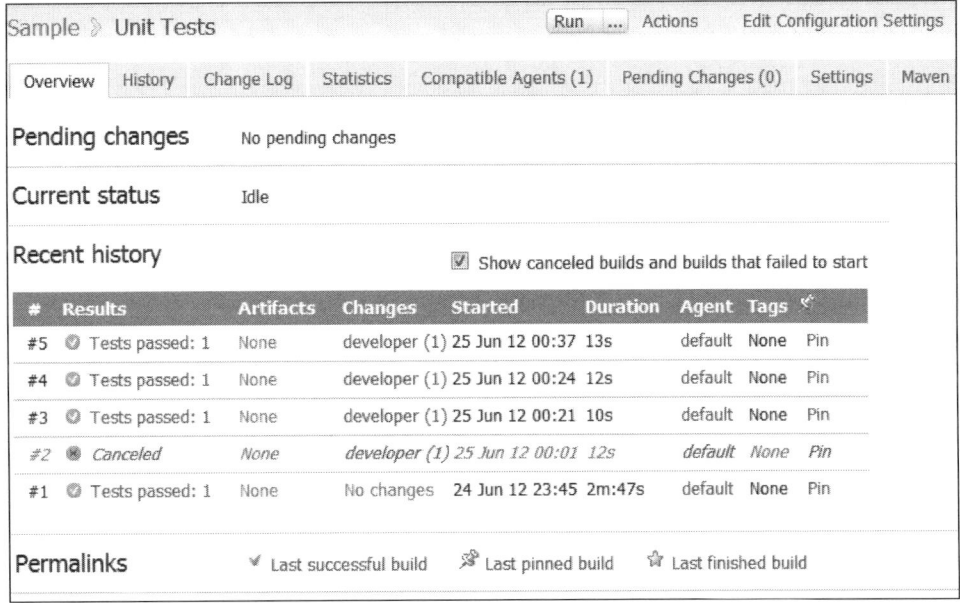

Configuring the TeamCity Server

You can click on an instance to find the correlated information in more detail.

To alter the settings of the current build configuration, click on the **Edit Configuration Settings** link in the top-right corner. This time you will not see a wizard but go right to the first (**General Settings**) step. Here you can directly select the configuration step that you'd like to update. Click on **Build Triggering**.

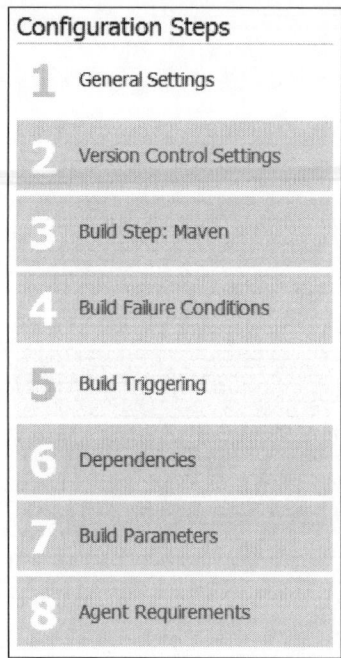

Click on the **Add new trigger** button and choose the **VCS Trigger** option:

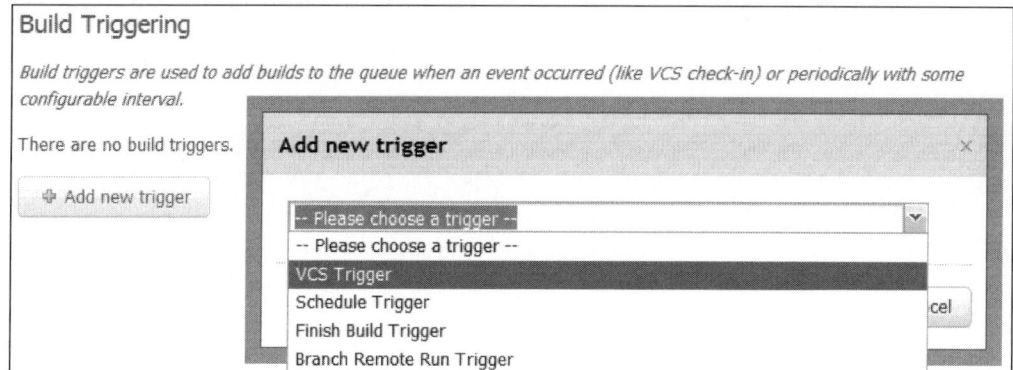

On the next screen, select the **Trigger a build on each check-in** checkbox, click on **Save** and you're done.

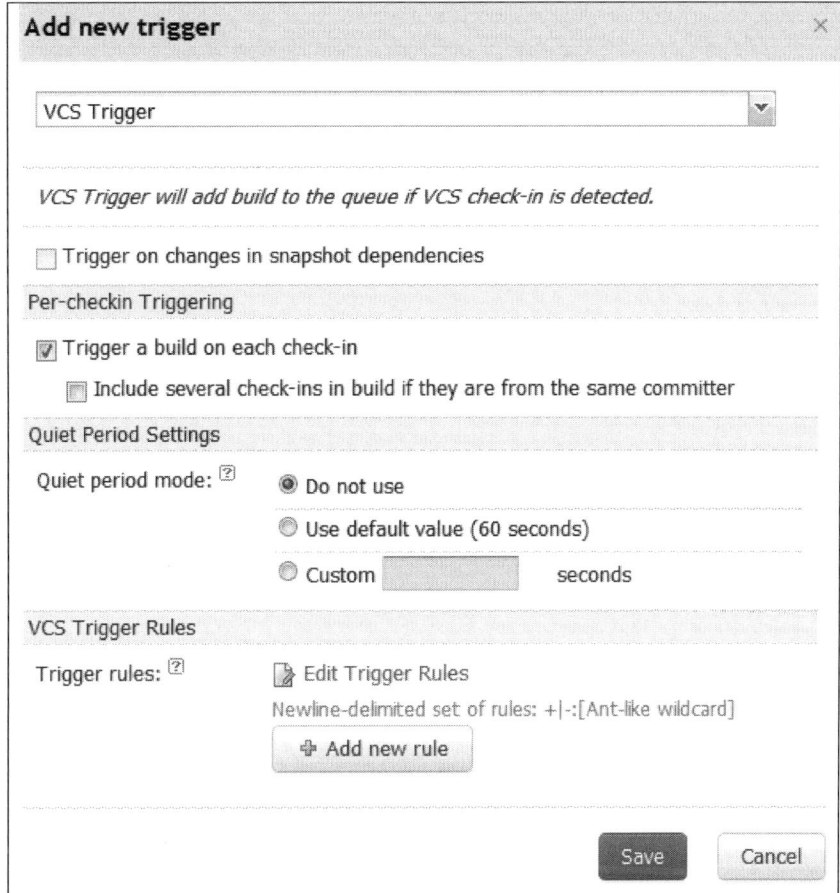

There are some other useful controls on this screen, for example, **Quiet Period Settings**. When enabled, whether for a default value or custom value, it will hold off immediate build triggering after commit. This command instructs TeamCity to wait for a customized period of time in case of some subsequent code changes that may come in.

Some developers tend to perform partial commits for whatever reasons. If check-ins are separated by a shorter period of time than the value of the quiet period, then only one ultimate build will be run for all these changes accumulated together in one go.

Configuring the TeamCity Server

Another pro of this feature is the fewer loads on the TeamCity server and its build agents as builds are run less often. The major con is that it's sometimes hard to tell who exactly has broken the build with which changes if several commits were run in one cumulative build.

After clicking on **Save,** your changes to the triggers are submitted and enabled at once.

Let's make sure our change has worked. Go to `CalculatorTest.java` and add this designedly failing test:

```
public void testBad() throws Exception {
    Assert.fail("Some bad test has failed");
}
```

Now commit your test and browse TeamCity's overview page.

At this point, TeamCity discovers that a change has been made to the source code and the trigger is fired and an automatic build is started.

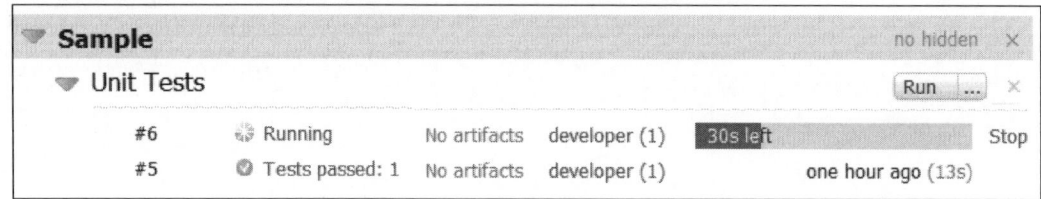

After a short period of time, the bad test fails and TeamCity reports the error.

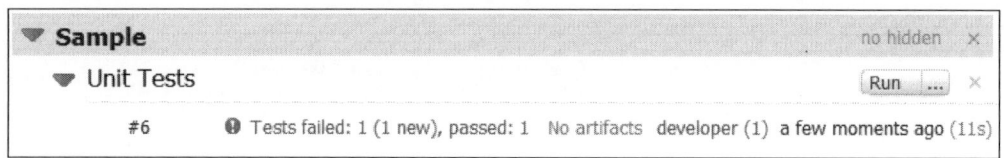

By taking a brief look, it can be seen that one test has failed; this test is new (did not fail in a previous build) and there's one good test that passed successfully. Clicking on this red link will redirect you to a page that provides detailed information concerning the fallen test(s).

To fully verify automaticity of our Continuous Integration process, replace the bad test with the following code and perform a commit:

```
public void testGood() throws Exception {
    Assert.assertTrue("This test should not fail", true);
}
```

In a matter of seconds, TeamCity will trigger a build for the code change in the corresponding VCS root, and all red banners placed on the overview page will be removed.

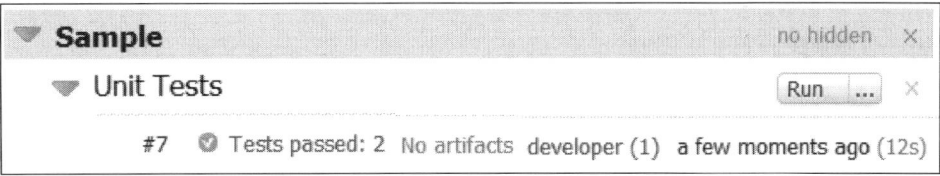

Configuring and maintaining the TeamCity server

Most general configuration options can be tweaked in the **Administration** area, which is only available to users with administrative privileges. Some fine tuning settings for the detailed internal working of TeamCity are hidden from the main site, and can be revealed with the help of information from the official TeamCity online administration guide found at http://confluence.jetbrains.net/display/TCD7/Administrator%27s+Guide.

This section is divided into several subsections. We'll go through most of them in brief and review user management later in more detail.

Project-related settings

When you go to the **Administration** area, you will see the **Projects** page in the **Project-related Settings** section displayed by default. Here you may get an overview of existing projects and their build configurations, and manage them all right away by clicking on the **edit** link. You can also start creating a new project or build configuration directly from here.

The next page is **VCS roots,** which shows all roots set up in TeamCity, and the projects to which they are attached. It is possible to edit them in one click or detach some root from its related project(s).

Next is **Build History Clean-up**. By default, TeamCity does not carry out any housekeeping. In other words, every bit of generated information such as statistics or build artifacts is kept forever and never removed. In case you are concerned about free disk space, the useful timed cleanup can be scheduled on this page. Settings may be configured on a per-project basis.

The last page in this section is **Audit**. This page shows a list of actions performed recently by every user. It could be very useful to know who has done what, where, and when.

Integrations

The first integration which may be handy is the one with **Issue Tracker**. Say you are using Atlassian JIRA and wish to integrate TeamCity with it. It's never been easier—merely click on **Create new connection**, select **JIRA** in the **Connection Type** drop-down box, and provide the required inputs. As a result, all builds containing specified JIRA tickets in the comments will get linked to the corresponding tickets. JIRA issue names will become clickable in every change list displayed on TeamCity, and will guide you right to the matching issues cited on the JIRA website.

The subsequent page is **Report Tabs**. Here you can state a build artifact URL, and provide the associated **Tab Title** string. If the **Project-level** report is used, the new tab will be added to this project's page. If the **Build-level** report is preferred, this tab will be added to the present tabs seen on the build overview page when the build produces this artifact.

NuGet Settings allows you to use the NuGet package manager to install or update NuGet packages, and to pack and publish packages to the desired feed.

Maven Settings allows you to upload Maven settings files to be used later in your builds executed by Maven. You may upload as many settings files as you wish and later deliberately use them as they get distinct names augmented with current date and time. These files appear in the **User settings** selection drop-down box on **Build Step: Maven configuration** stage for all projects that make use of Maven.

The **Tools** page shows the platform-dependent tools used by TeamCity to control the workflow for the server and build agents, for detecting locked files in the checkout directory, or pushing installation files to the Windows host and executing them remotely from the Windows server.

Server administration

This section includes major settings for server configuration. The **Global settings** page collects general settings which are pretty self-descriptive. An interesting option for us here is **Registration on the login page**, which is described in the next section along with **Email** and **Jabber notifier**. Advanced server configuration will be reviewed in *Chapter 7, Advanced Configuration*.

The **Agent Cloud** page enables integration with Amazon EC2 Cloud. In short, you may outsource your build agents' hardware facilities to Amazon cloud in order to satisfy vast varying demands for hardware resources, which could undergo rapid unexpected growth. During and just before releases, high loads of tests and builds become a common matter. So, why not push them into the mighty cloud? For additional information on how to accomplish this, please visit the manual located at http://www.jetbrains.com/teamcity/features/amazon_ec2.html.

On the **Diagnostics** page, you may tweak some internal properties, which mostly speak for themselves. Most of them do not require immediate attention and can be researched later.

Backup and restore will be discussed later in this book.

The **Licenses** page contains information about your existing licenses, and provides the ability to add a new one with a corresponding button.

The **Usage Statistics** page displays historical data collected throughout the lifetime of the TeamCity server. This could be useful in order to customize TeamCity for more efficient performance in future.

Last, but definitely not the least, is the **Plugins list** page. On this page there's a massive list of plugins that come bundled with TeamCity. If you cannot find the desired plugin here, you may browse an even longer list of plugins by clicking on the associated link atop the page. There you can find other useful plugins (or a somewhat unusual plugin such as Fools Day plugin). If there's still no luck finding the plugin of your choice, you may write your own using the new and improved OpenAPI.

Maintaining users and their permissions

The easiest way to create a user account on TeamCity is to let the user create it on his own. TeamCity supports the auto-registration feature for new users, which can be enabled in the **Administration** panel. If you are adopting Continuous Integration via TeamCity over an existing project with many people, the better choice would be letting users create their accounts, and provide credentials such as e-mail ID and password right on the welcome page. It is possible to change their details or assign administrator roles to them later.

To enable this feature, you should have an administrator role. Go to **Administration | Server Administration | Global Settings** and check the corresponding box named **Registration on the login page**.

Configuring the TeamCity Server

There are more global user-related controls on this page, such as the customizable welcome text on the login page. Some advanced user configurations will be discussed later in *Chapter 7, Advanced Configuration*. Also, you can enable guest logins which require no authorization and establish a guest username (by default it's `guest`). The rest of the user and group associated settings are in the **User Management** tab of the **Administration** page. Let's go add a dedicated record for our developer which we're using to work with an SVN of the same name, `developer`.

Go to **Administration | User Management | Users**.

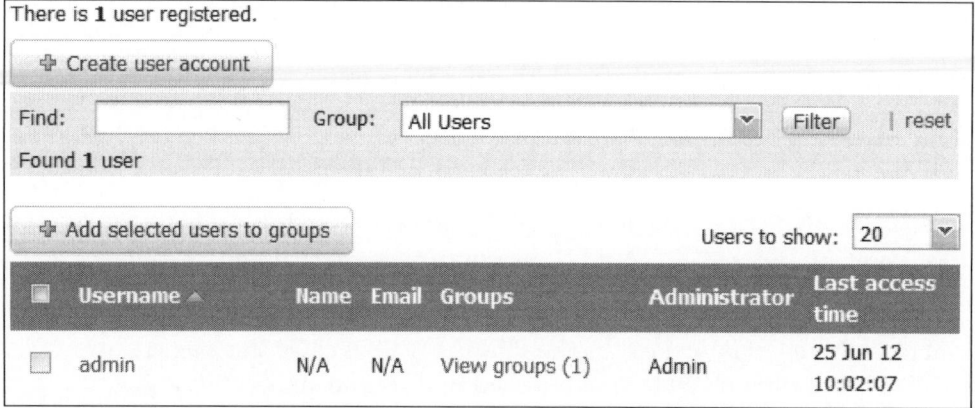

You can see that now there's only one user registered and it is an admin user. Let's add a new user. To do so, click on the **Create user account** button.

Here you need to provide a username and password. You can also set this user as an administrator if you wish. The last checkbox is useful when you need to create a bunch of users at once and stay on this page after submitting the form. Otherwise you are sent to the users' overview page where you'll see a confirmation—**User "developer" has been created successfully**. You may also check the list of users which now consists of two records.

You may now try to log in as a newly created user to see his environment. If you open TeamCity in another browser and provide the `developer` user's credentials, you are going to see something like this:

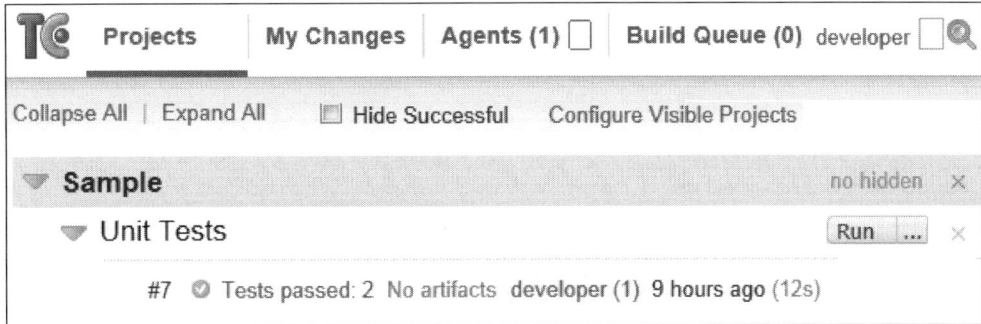

As you can see, the **Administration** link is gone and the name now shows **developer**. Now if you visit the **My Changes** tab, you'll see that TeamCity has bound SVN's user with current user, **developer**, via username and aggregated all his changes on that tab. If you go to the **My Changes** tab under admin account, you're going to see that no changes have been collected for this user (remember, we've done commits to SVN under the `developer` username).

Should you be willing to apply some settings to many users at once or configure some common permissions, it is achievable through **Groups** found in **Administration | User Management**. There is already one group named **All Users,** which contains all TeamCity users and cannot be deleted itself, and also cannot exclude any users. Every user you create on TeamCity falls under this group by default and stays there until you totally delete him.

Configuring notifications

So it looks like we are all set up. We have the build configuration in place, which will either succeed or fail and display a detailed explanation on the web interface. We have users with permissions to trigger build configurations, and for some to even alter its settings. But didn't we forget something? How would anyone know that the build has failed? By checking its status on TeamCity's powerful web application—someone may say. But many would argue with this statement as people are sometimes too lazy to check each commit, or may be excessively busy or even unaware of those automatic builds happening somewhere. In order to apply CI successfully, each and every change in the source base simply cannot go unnoticed.

Without ongoing notifications, the power of Continuous Integration will die in vain. So please ensure that every step off the path triggers a big red message sent by whichever means to every party that may be interested in the success of the whole project. Putting managers in the mailing list is a good way to ensure that a broken build will not stay so for a long time (joke).

There is an extensive amount of notification options supported by TeamCity. Let's go through them in brief.

E-mail

This is a must-have, and the most commonly used preference. It is worth setting it up from the very beginning and later complimenting it with other available options. A good practice is creating a very general e-mail notification rule that triggers a warning should something go wrong. This rule then could be applied to all projects and assigned it to the **All Users** group in the system.

IDE

For this instant notification option, the supported IDEs are Jetbrains' own IntelliJ IDEA and Eclipse. This notification, once configured, will always keep you in touch with the general build status and your particular changes. Should the build fail the red icon on the IDE's bottom panel and optional pop-up window won't let you miss anything urgent.

Windows tray

It is a nice immediate option available for Windows only. Useful to be set up on machines where there is no actual IDE installed at all (could be useful for QAs or management and so on). Also there's a minor possibility that the used IDE is not supported by related IDE notification plugins yet.

Jabber/XMPP

It is possible to send plain text notification messages via Jabber. All settings are done on the **Jabber Notifier** page at **Administration | Server Administration**.

Atom/RSS feed

This choice is configured in a separate and different way from previous ones. You need to create a template in FreeMarker Template Language and place it in `TeamCity data directory/config/feed-item-template.ftl`. Under the same directory there's a default template, `default-feed-item-template.ftl`, which can be used as an example. Please do not place your edits in this default file because it gets overwritten at each server startup.

Already preinstalled configurations

Browse to **Administration | User | Groups**, click on the **All Users** group, and go to the **Notification Rules** tab.

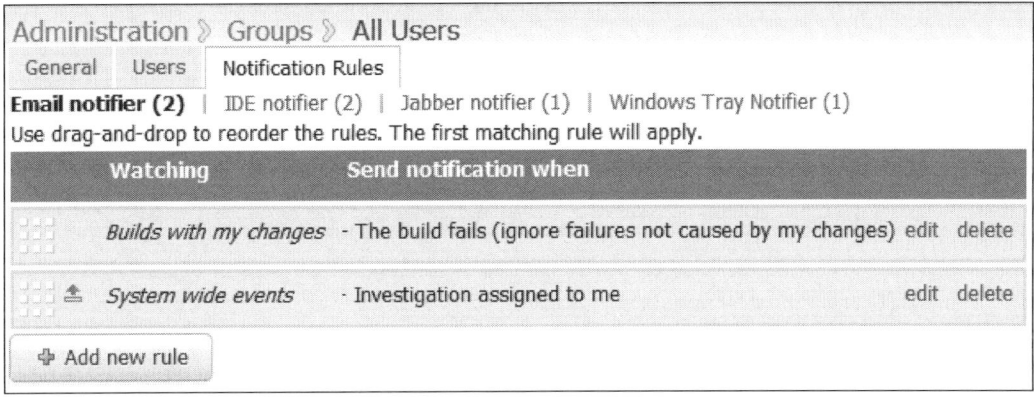

You can see that there are already **2** e-mail notifier configurations pre-created for you. To make it work, the interested user should have a valid e-mail provided in their profile and a proper e-mail server should be configured at **Administration | Server Administration | Email Notifier**.

Adding custom notification rules

Let's create a new general rule which will suit our needs. Go back to the **All Users** group, select the **Notification Rules** tab, and click on the **Add new rule** button.

You may select checkboxes as shown in the following screenshot:

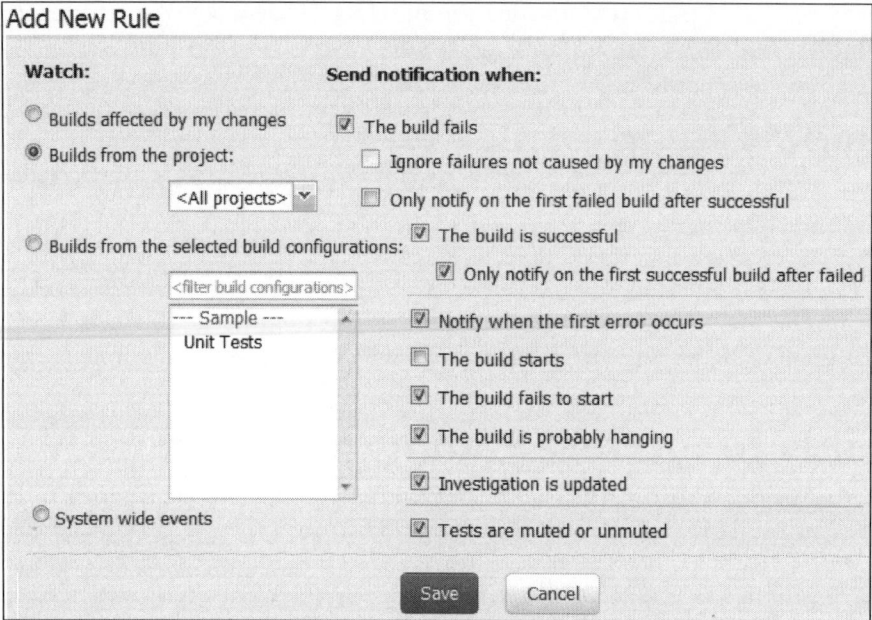

Every setting is pretty self-descriptive and should not require individual explanation.

Upon submitting, you should see your new rule added beneath two existing ones. You can either drag it higher using a mouse, or click on the small up arrow icon near the new configuration named **All projects**. This will ensure that your rule will be used first, as only first matching rule will win and stop event propagation further down the list.

From now on, every user who is registered on TeamCity with an appropriate e-mail will stay in touch with all events and news from the TeamCity server.

Summary

In this chapter, we have set up our project to be automatically built and tested on every commit to source control using TeamCity. From now on, no single breaking change to the source code will go unnoticed. Any interested party can get access to the latest news about the total status, and may go further into the details when needed.

Even if you are not a developer and do not have IDE, you may keep abreast of what's going on by means of customizable e-mails and the Windows system tray notifier.

5
Integration with an IDE

Earlier we saw how TeamCity executes code irrespective of the IDE. It is always possible not to have an IDE at all and still apply Continuous Integration with TeamCity. You can write code in the simplest text editor, commit it via a command-line client, and be happy seeing your results, whether good or not so good, on your web application. The only problem here is that too many obstacles arise between you and your program. Making use of an IDE lets you write faster, be more effective, and work with additional comfort. If you can imagine how much more you get writing code in an IDE compared to not using it, you may get an idea about how much extra comfort you are receiving when working with an IDE that is natively supported by TeamCity.

At the time of writing, TeamCity supports IntelliJ IDEA by Jetbrains (written by the same company who created TeamCity), a very popular Eclipse IDE, and not to forget Microsoft Visual Studio (sorry NetBeans, you are less lucky).

In this chapter, you'll know how to:

- Install the TeamCity integration plugin into IntelliJ IDEA
- Install the TeamCity plugin for Eclipse
- Start working and using the TeamCity plugin

IntelliJ IDEA

As it is the product of the same company, it gets maximum support and interconnection. Both, the free community edition and the paid ultimate edition, get the same level of backing, which provides exclusive control of every change in the code.

Installing from the plugins repository

Follow these steps to install TeamCity from the plugins repository:

1. Installation of the TeamCity plugin into IntelliJ IDEA is pretty easy and straightforward. If you have an Internet connection, then in IDEA, go to **File | Settings | Plugins | Browse repositories** and search for `TeamCity Integration`.

   > At the time of writing, the supported version of TeamCity is 7.0. In case you are using a version older than 7.0, go and install it anyway. Then, on the first login to TeamCity, you will be offered to automatically get the plugin updated to the proper version by the TeamCity server.

2. Right-click on the plugin shown in the list and select **Download and Install**. Accept the confirmation box that appears, wait until the plugin is downloaded, and click on **OK** in the **Browse Repositories** window. After that, click on **OK** in the **Settings** window and either accept immediate restart or postpone it until required.

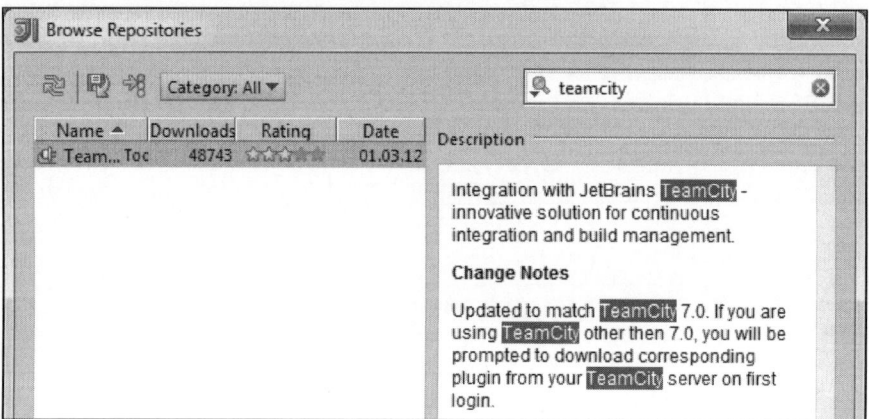

Installing from the TeamCity server

Sometimes, at the development environment box, the Internet is not available or may be too restricted to make the previous approach work. Don't worry, the TeamCity installation bundle has taken care of it.

1. Log in to the TeamCity server, go to **My Settings & Tools** (available via clicking on the small "expand" arrow to the right of your name.

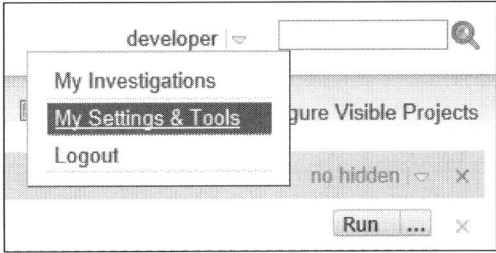

2. On the right, you are presented with the specific plugins for supported IDEs.

3. Click on the **download** link near **IntelliJ Platform plugin** and download `TeamCity-IDEAplugin.zip` to your local machine.
4. After this, in IDEA, go to **File | Settings | Plugins | Install plugin from disk** and in the file explorer window, browse to the previously downloaded ZIP archive. If you do not have plugins for specific version control systems (in enabled state) on which the TeamCity plugin has a dependency, you would get a warning and be asked to enable those necessary disabled plugins.

5. Then click on **OK** to submit the **Plugins** window, and select whether you wish to perform restart later or at once, in order to activate the changes in plugins.

Integration in action

Now let's see how we can benefit from using the TeamCity plugin installed in our integrated development environment.

IntelliJ IDEA

Take notice of the new TeamCity tool window that appeared in IDEA's bottom-left corner. In the bottom-right corner of the IDEA status bar, you may find a new TeamCity status icon—a light-blue colored circle with two red dots on it. This particular icon means that IDEA is not currently connected to the TeamCity server. It's time to establish a connection.

1. In IDEA click on **TeamCity** in the top menu and then log in.

2. Enter your credentials, uncheck the **Use IDEA proxy settings** checkbox if you are not using a proxy to access TeamCity and click on **OK**. After quite a few seconds, the status bar circle icon changes to green "check" icon.

3. If you hover your mouse over the icon, you'll see a message confirming that you are successfully connected to the TeamCity server with the username **developer**. If you click on the green "check" icon, you'll see a new TeamCity tool window.

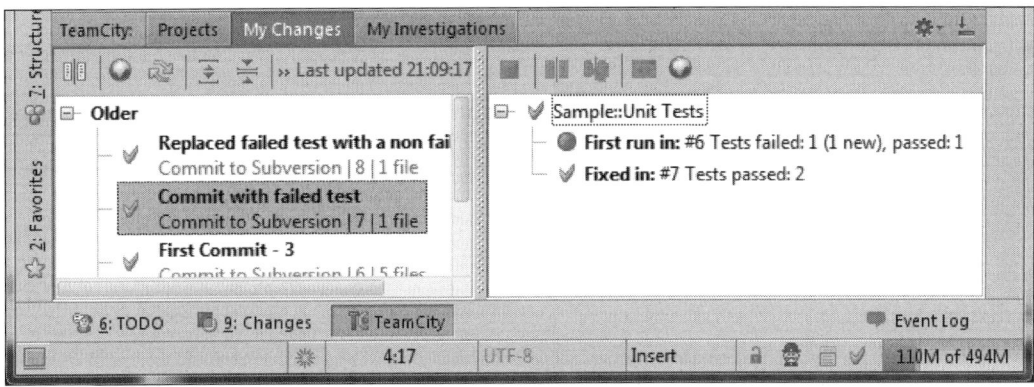

There you can find a tabular layout analogous to that on the TeamCity web application. Here you have **Projects**, **My Changes,** and a new **My Investigations** tab (on the webapp, the latter one is hidden in the drop-down menu near your username at the top-right corner). In the **My Changes** tab, you can find all the changes that made their way through TeamCity by your user (by username). It is possible to instantly view all changes associated with specific commit- or open-related TeamCity web application page in the browser.

On the **Projects** tab, there's a button to configure visible projects (it actually redirects you to the browser), following is an instant add-build-to-queue button along with one to view the pending changes owned by you. Pending changes get populated when you've committed something, but TeamCity did not process those changes yet.

Integration with an IDE

> The **My Investigations** technique is used to track down the research for culprits of failed builds or such. When you start "investigating" some problem through the TeamCity web application in this tab, you'll see a list of all the investigations you are involved in and their status. To bring up full log information for that build in a new tab at any given moment, you may double-click a particular build results list item. This technique works in the **Projects** tab as well.

In the next chapter, you'll know how to use one of the most useful and outstanding TeamCity features — the remote run (pre-tested commit). This feature lets you run tests before performing an actual commit, thus shielding the project sources in your VCS from broken code / resource changes being committed.

Eclipse

In a way similar to the one for IntelliJ IDEA to perform the installation in Eclipse, you need to download the necessary plugin from the TeamCity web application.

1. Go to **My Settings & Tools** | **TeamCity Tools**, right-click on the **update site link** URL under **Eclipse Plugin**, and select the **Copy shortcut** option (or any similar option) in the browser's drop-down menu. Now you have the required link copied into the system clipboard.

2. Next, in Eclipse go to **Help** | **Install New Software** | **Add**.

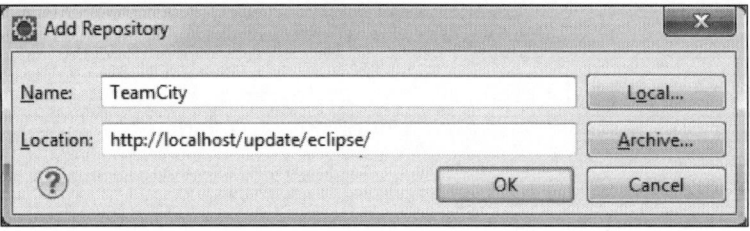

3. Provide **Name** (`TeamCity`), paste the repository URL location from the clipboard (copied at the previous step) to the **Location** field, and click on **OK**.

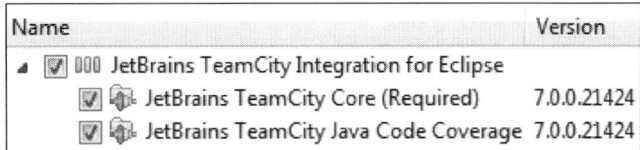

4. Back on the **Install** screen, check the checkboxes for TeamCity features and click on the **Next** button. Accept the offered license agreement and restart Eclipse.

5. After restart, you will see, at the bottom-right corner of Eclipse's status bar, two new icons added by the TeamCity plugin.

6. The status message over the icon says that you are currently not logged in. Now right-click on the right-most blue icon and select **Login** in the appearing menu.

Integration with an IDE

7. Enter your credentials here along with the TeamCity server URL and click on **OK**. In a few seconds, TeamCity will be connected and the icon will change to a green check mark. TeamCity integration adds two more extra views to Eclipse—**TeamCity Watched Projects** and **TeamCity My Changes**.

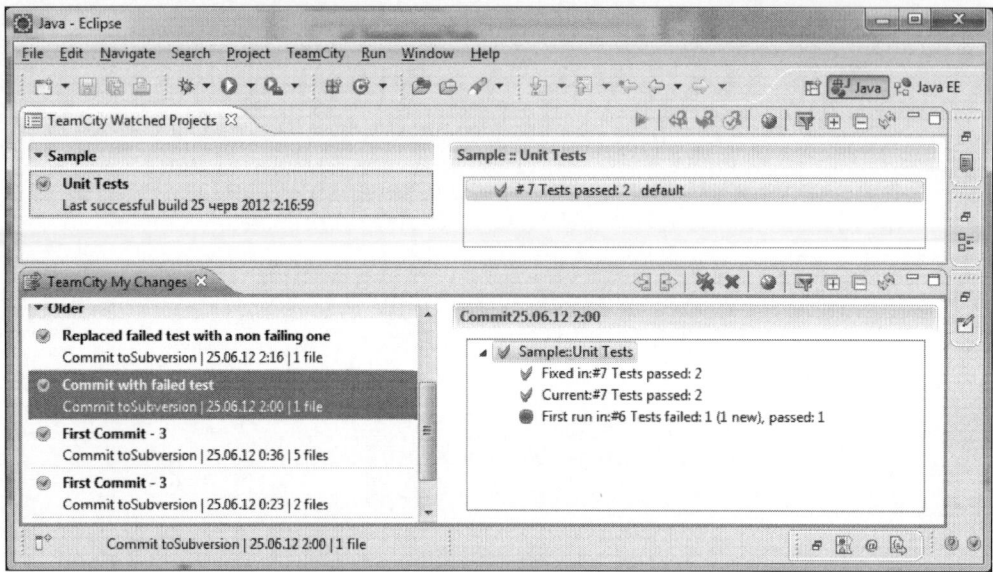

TeamCity Watched Projects shows the current status of all supervised projects and allows instant adding of selected build to the running queue. Also investigation controls are available here.

With the **TeamCity My Changes** view, you may observe the status of all your changes. Double-clicking on any particular build result (this also works in the **Watched Projects** view) will open up full log information for that build.

Summary

At this point, we have a powerful integration of our IDE with the TeamCity server, which after a short configuration allows us not to visit the server's web application anymore. Everything comes at hand with no major efforts from our side. To either run a build or stop it, and to research the full build log, there's no need to leave your comfortable IDE. You may even review every change done by you merely in several clicks right from the IDE. Now you can hold the great power of Continuous Integration provided by TeamCity in the palm of your hand.

In the next chapter, you will learn how to execute a remote run on TeamCity. We will organize multiple projects with templates and create a chained multi-step build.

6
Enhanced Techniques

If you've read this far and are still interested, then TeamCity should definitely suit your needs. In this chapter, you'll know some additional advanced techniques which are going to help you a lot when applying Continuous Integration via TeamCity's services.

In this chapter you'll know how to:

- Do a remote run in IntelliJ IDEA and Eclipse
- Organize multiple projects with templates
- Create multi-step builds

Remote run

This is, truly, the best technique, second only to automatic builds happening after changes are detected. The idea behind it is that it would be great if your code change has been checked against all tests, not after the actual commit, but in fact, just before it. It would keep the version control system contents clean, not only of non-compilable code, but also from broken tests and resources forgotten to be committed (keep in mind that in case tests are really weak and do not actually test anything, neither TeamCity nor any other build tool will help your project to stay in good shape). You can take a quick look at the green "check" icon in the IDE status bar and be sure that the project is capable of using the `dev` environment for testing.

Let's see how it could work with our sample project. An effective example may be adding new business logic into our calculator, and then testing it with the corresponding test.

Enhanced Techniques

1. Open `Calculator.java` created in *Chapter 2, Sample Project*, and add a brand new operation, a `multiply` method. Let's pretend that we act as a usual developer who copy-pastes an already existing `sum` method to save some time and does not write a new one from scratch. Every so often, the programmer merely alters the name of the new method and forgets to update the actual contents. This is how `Calculator.java` now looks like:

   ```
   package com.packtpub;
   public class Calculator {
       public int sum(int x, int y) {
           return x + y;
       }
       public int multiply(int x, int y) {
           return x + y;
       }
   }
   ```

2. Then the software engineer knows that the test should be written for the business logic. So he adds into `CalculatorTest.java` the next test, replacing the existing dummy test that always passes.

   ```
   public void testMultiply() throws Exception {
       Calculator calculator = new Calculator();
       int product = calculator.multiply(2, 3);
       Assert.assertEquals(6, product);
   }
   ```

3. As you may have guessed, this test will not pass. This could be figured out either through the local launching of this test or from the e-mail that everyone gets from TeamCity after running broken build. Let's assume that the given test boasts a pretty heavy load on the local machine making simultaneous development impossible. Or the situation could be that you need to use some remote database for the test and the connection is very slow now — in other words, there's some reason forcing you not to run the test locally.

4. Being a careful developer, the do-commit-and-see-if-it-works approach seems unacceptable. But what does the programmer have to do then? And here comes the time when remote run steps in. This feature allows you to test your changes before performing the actual commit. It is possible to schedule the changes to be committed automatically should they pass the check on TeamCity.

IntelliJ IDEA

In order to make remote run work in IntelliJ IDEA, follow these steps:

1. From the top menu select **VCS | Commit Changes**.

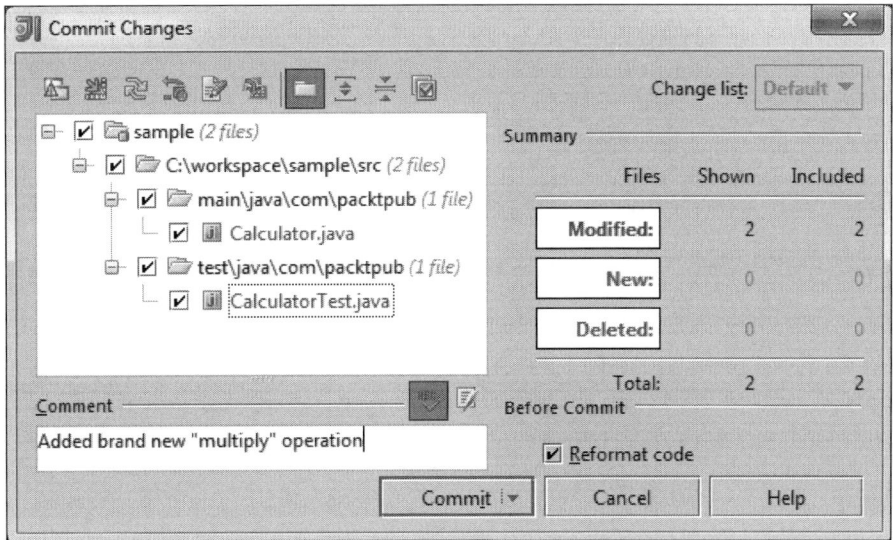

2. Note the small down arrow near the **Commit** button. If you expand, it you will find that there is a new available action, **Remote Run...**.

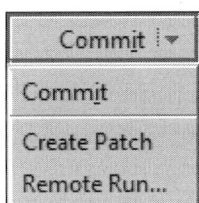

 The same action is possible by selecting **TeamCity | Remote Run** in **IDEA** menu.

3. Now, a detailed **Remote Run** window is opened. During the first launch of this window, you need to check the build configurations against which you wish to schedule remote run.

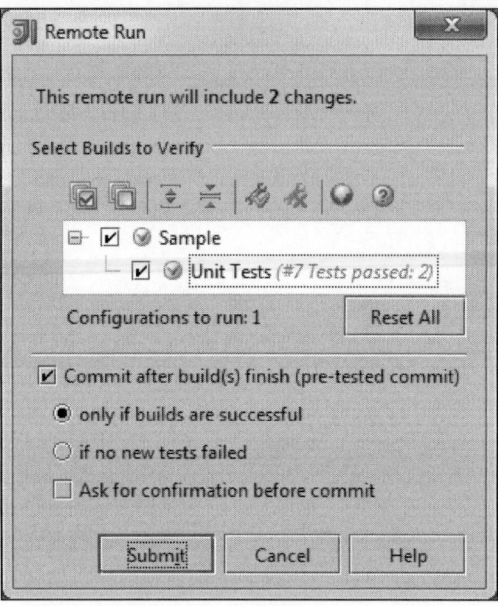

4. If you want TeamCity to perform automatic commit after finishing the build, check the related checkbox. There are two available preconditions that should be met for committing.
    - The first and more restrictive option requires that the build should be successful—meaning no compromise, code should compile, and all tests should pass.
    - The second option passes a commit through if there are no new tests failed by this build (in other words there could already be some failed ones).

The last checkbox being set will command IDEA to raise a confirmation box upon successful build, asking you whether you are okay if your code would now be committed because TeamCity is now OK with it.

5. Let's click on **Submit** and watch what happens.

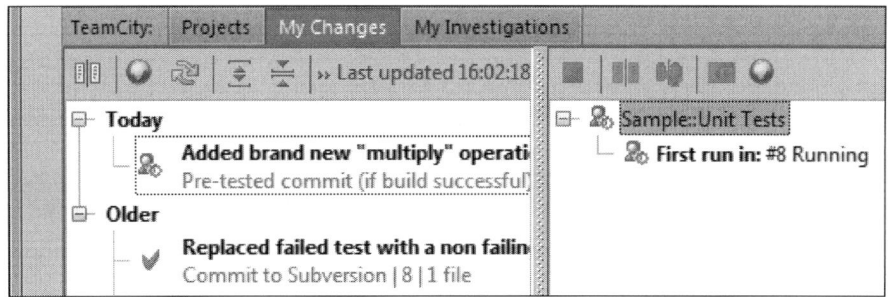

6. If we go right away to the TeamCity tool window and browse to the **My Changes** tab, we will see that our personal remote run build is running currently. As expected, it will not succeed and in a matter of seconds, you will get alerts at the top-right corner of your working environment in IDEA.

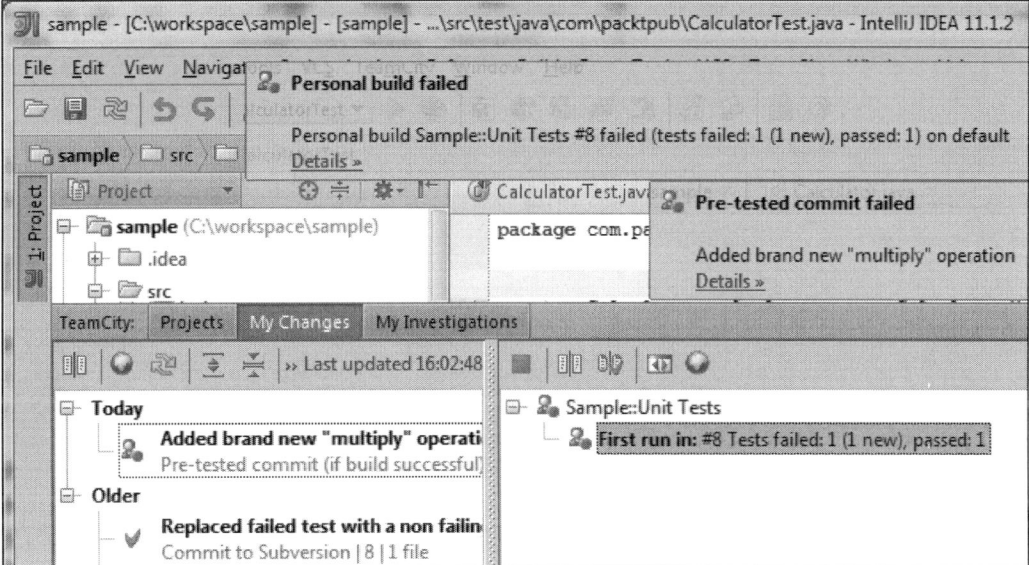

Enhanced Techniques

7. We can see here in **My Changes** that one new test has failed and one has passed fine. Two upper pop-up notifications show us that the personal build has failed and thereafter, the pre-tested commit has failed altogether. If you double-click on the test report string in the bottom-right box (or click on the **Details** link on the **Personal build failed** pop-up window), you'll get the detailed information about your failed test.

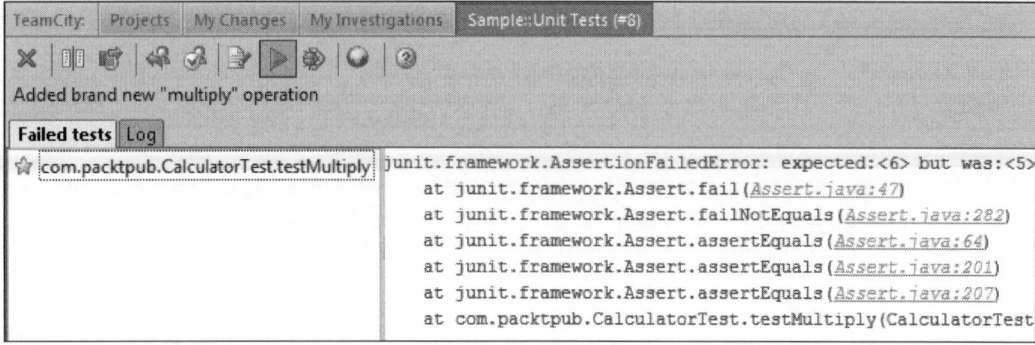

You will see a log message for the failed test as it was run on your local machine. If there were multiple tests failing, there would be more records on the left, each containing details for the associated test.

The main point for remote run should be clearly evident now—there is no broken code in **Version Control System** (**VCS**), failed logic did not get its way through TeamCity, and as long as remote run is "personal", no one else will be worried and bothered by e-mails with lots of red text from TeamCity (except the author of the remote run).

8. Now let's see how remote run works for a positive change. In IDEA, go to the **Changes** tool window and open the **Local** tab. There you may find a new change set added to **Default** with a name similar to the comment of your intended commit. This new change-set has been created by IDEA automatically to collect, non-committed personal build. It is easier to pinpoint the problem amongst a smaller of files and as usual, the problem is located in the new updates rather than in old unchanged files.

9. Right-click on the new change-set name and choose **Commit Changes**. As before, expand the arrow near the **Commit** button and choose **Remote Run**. Leave all the controls intact and click on **Submit**.

In several seconds, IDEA will show the commit progress bar by which we can tell that our remote run has just succeeded.

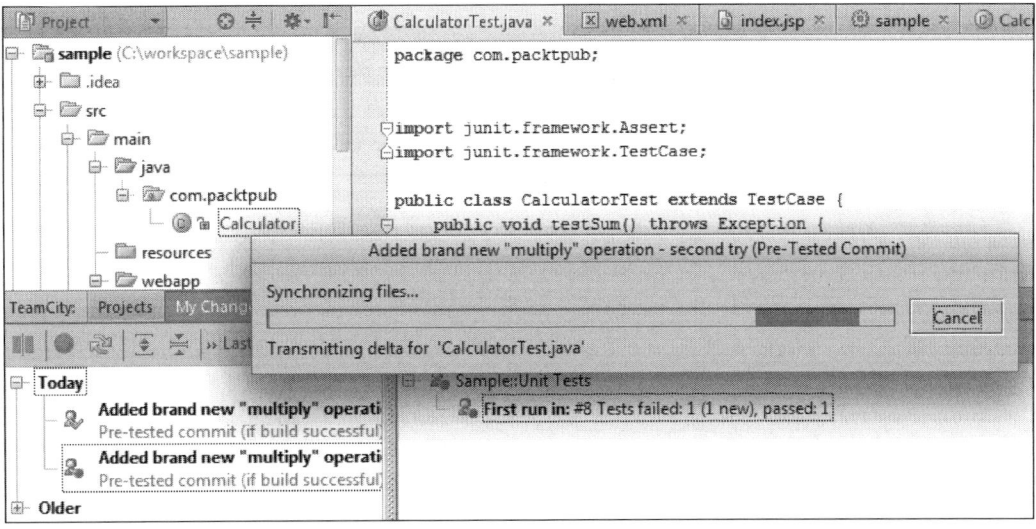

10. Within seconds, the commit process is completed and after a while, TeamCity will run an automatic build once more, as it detects a change in SVN (usually short name for Subversion repository). The **My Changes** tab is very informative, as it shows all builds from the current user. You may see the red personal delayed commit that broke the build (we've already reviewed it earlier). Then there are two green ones:

    ◦ The former being personal (and it shows on its icon a "person" near the green check mark)
    ◦ The latter one is a status message of TeamCity's automated build run after code check-in

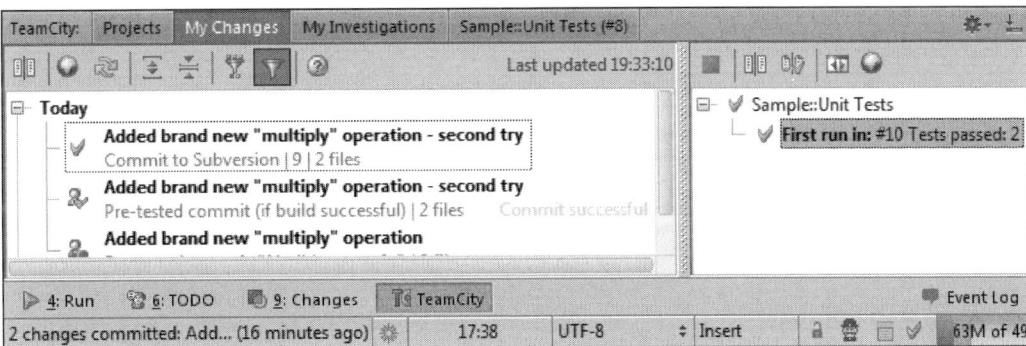

Eclipse

In order to make remote run work in Eclipse, you first need to install a plugin for Subversion support. This could be Subclipse or Subversive. Ensure that you are connected to the Internet because either option requires a working Internet connection.

1. Suppose we choose Subversive. In this case, in Eclipse, go to **Install New Software** in the menu **Help**. On the **Install** screen, expand the **Work with** drop-down list and look for **Subversive**. If it is not present, add its update site manually by clicking on the **Add** button and providing the proper URL (at the time of writing it is http://download.eclipse.org/technology/subversive/0.7/update-site/). Check the required feature named **Subversive SVN Team Provider (Incubation)** and click on **Next**.

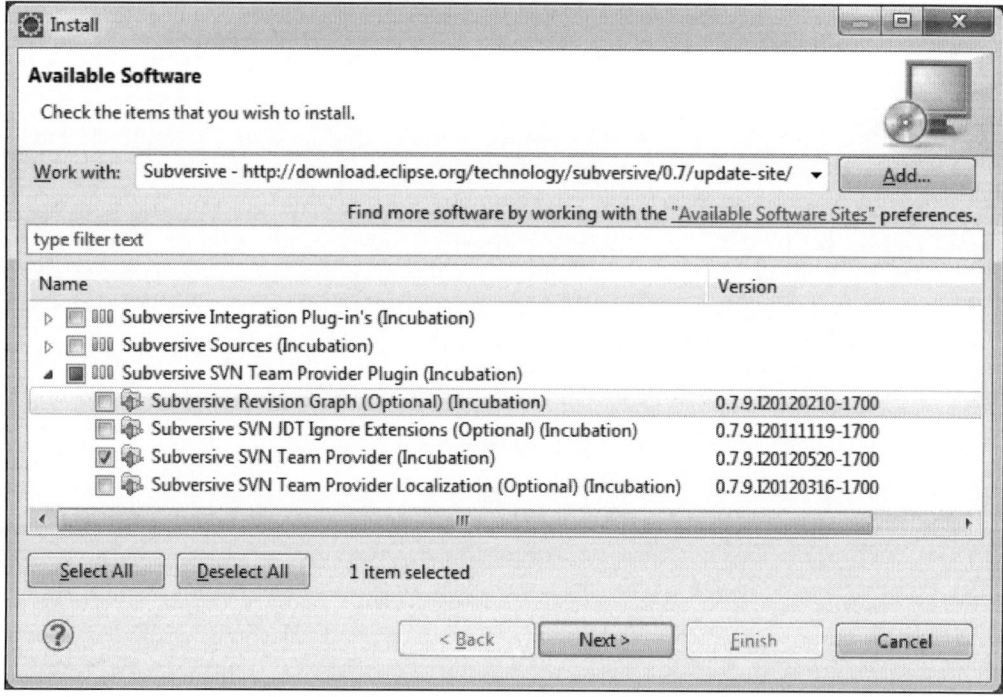

2. On the **Install Details** screen, click on **Next** once again.

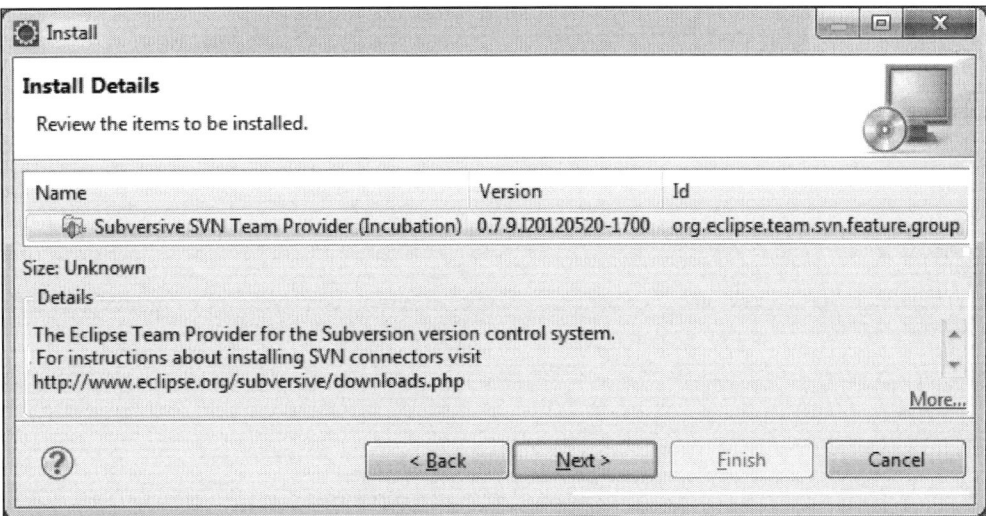

3. Then accept the license agreement, click on **Finish,** and finally restart Eclipse when it asks for it. After restart, you need to choose an appropriate SVN connector.

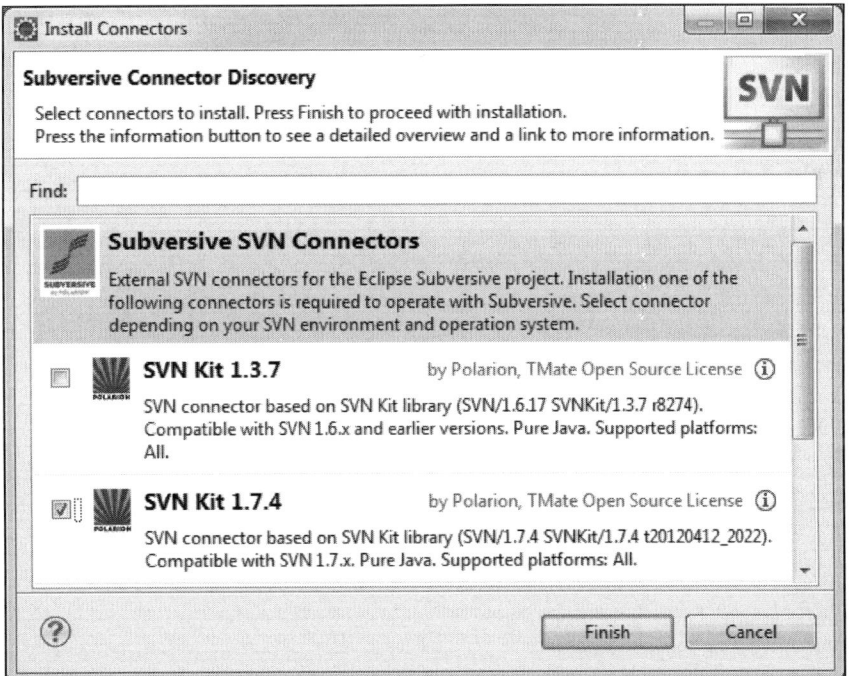

Enhanced Techniques

4. As our Subversion server uses Version 1.7, we select the second option. On the next **Install** screen, check all the required software and click on **Next**.

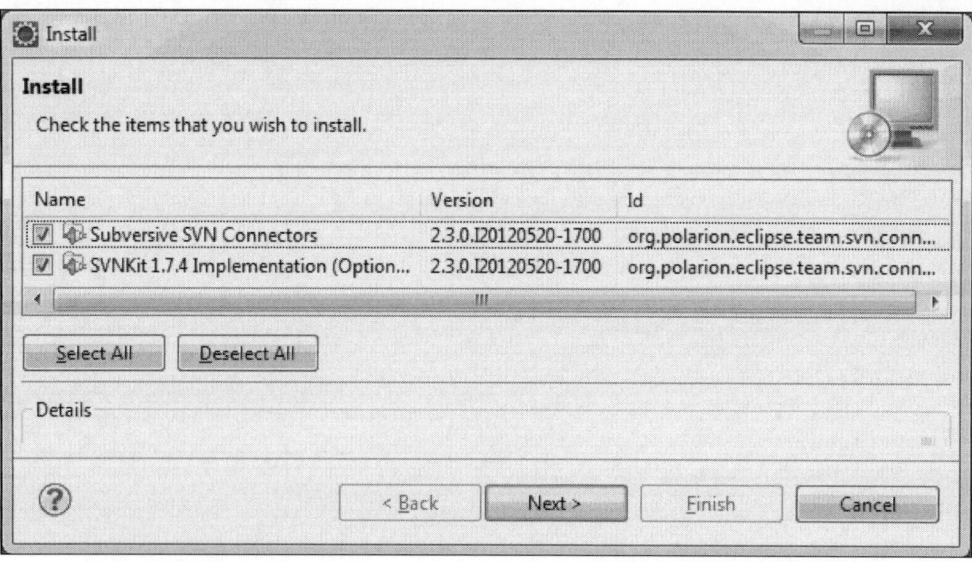

5. On the next confirmation screen, click on **Next** once again, then accept the terms of license agreement and click on **Finish**. Confirm the warning for untrusted content and click on **OK**. Restart Eclipse once again.

6. Now let's import a project from Subversion. In Eclipse, go to **File** | **Import** | **SVN** | **Project from SVN**. Click on **Create a new repository location** and then click on **Next**. Enter the proper URL (for example `https://svnserver:1443/svn/repo/sample/trunk`), username, and password. Click on **Next**.

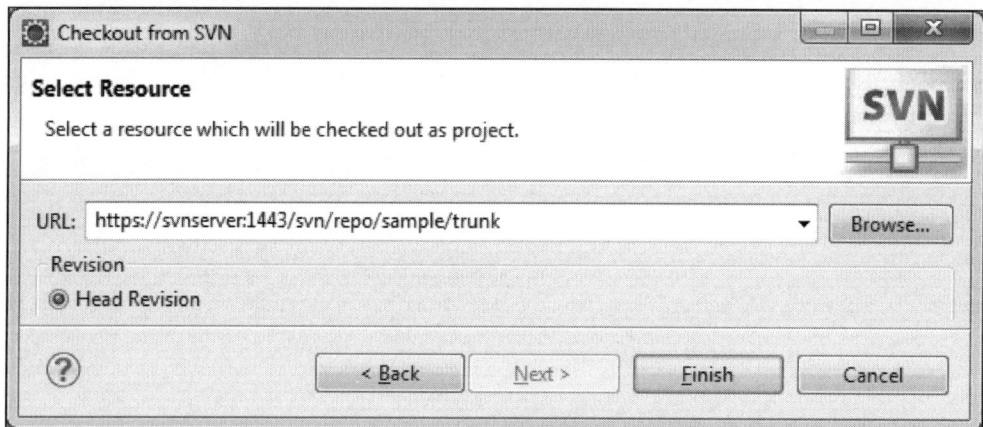

Chapter 6

7. Keep **Head Revision** selected and click on **Finish**. On the **Check Out As** screen, select **Check out as a project** with the name specified.

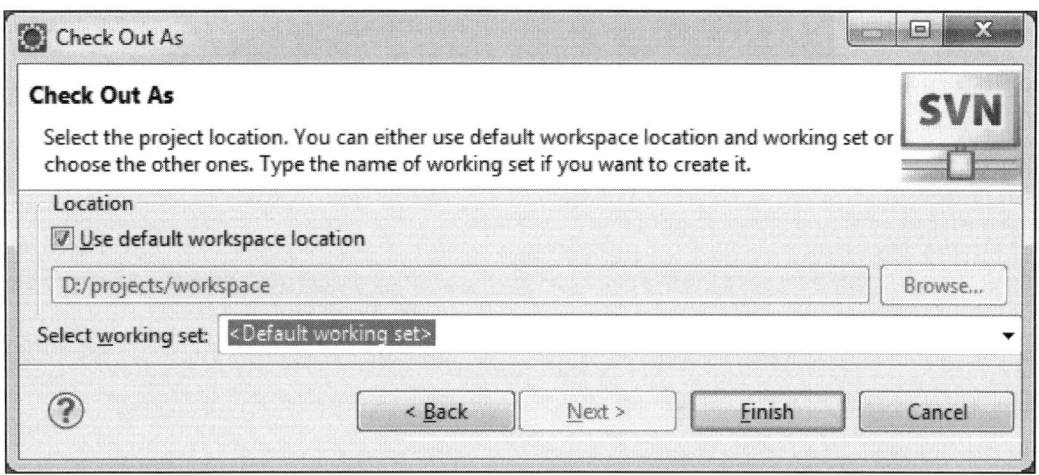

8. Click on **Next**, check the **Use default workspace location** checkbox, and finally click on **Finish**.

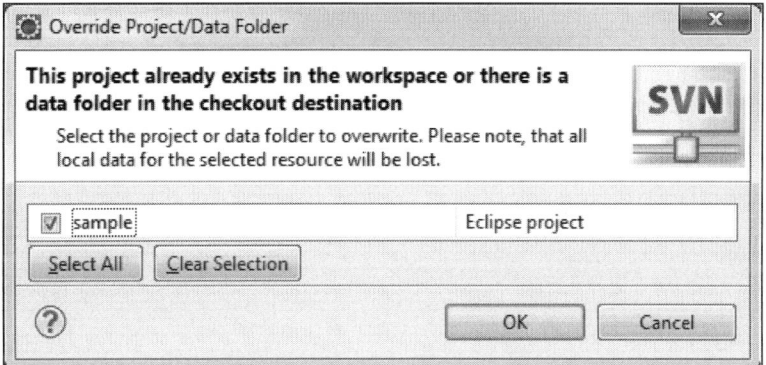

9. Eclipse will raise a warning saying that all your unsaved changes would be overwritten—but as we did not introduce any updates yet, we can go for it.

   Having finished the installation and configuration of the SVN plugin, you may follow the same path as with IDEA. From the top menu, select **TeamCity | Remote Run** and follow the same procedure from IDEA.

Organizing multiple projects with templates

It often happens that multiple comparable project configurations which should go in parallel need to be created and maintained at the same time. There is a simple way to create a similar project with minor differences without having to create it and set up all of its tedious settings from scratch. In TeamCity, this action is called "copy". With administrator privileges, you may copy any given project configuration to a new one.

Working with our sample project, we might need to separate our single build into two—a development build running against unit tests, and a deployment build running without unit tests but producing packaged a WAR file at the end.

Copying the project

In the first step, let's copy our existing build.

1. Go to the TeamCity web application, and click on **Administration**. You will be redirected directly to **Project-related Settings | Projects**.

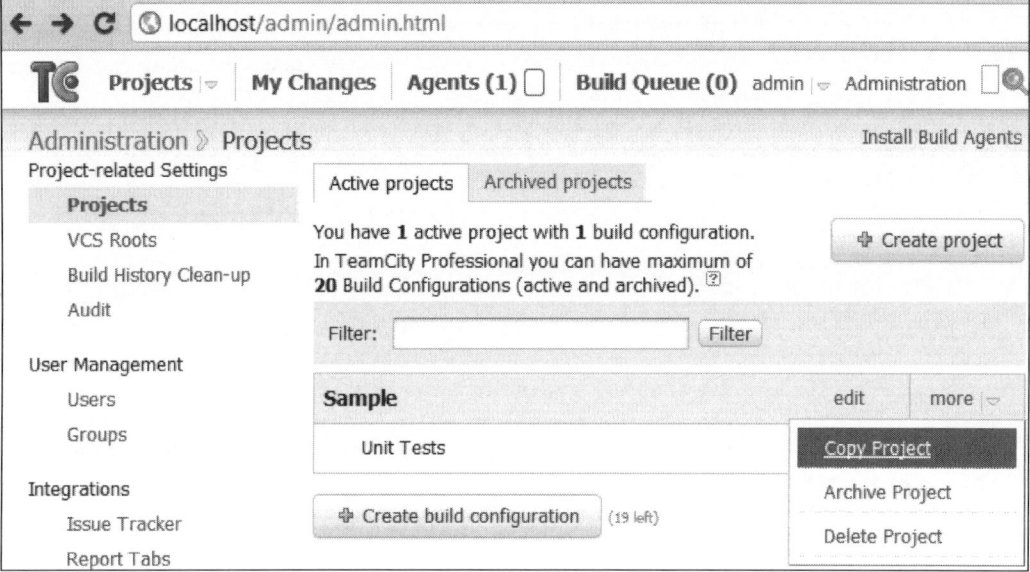

2. Find the expandable **more** link near the **Sample** project name and select **Copy Project** from the drop-down menu.

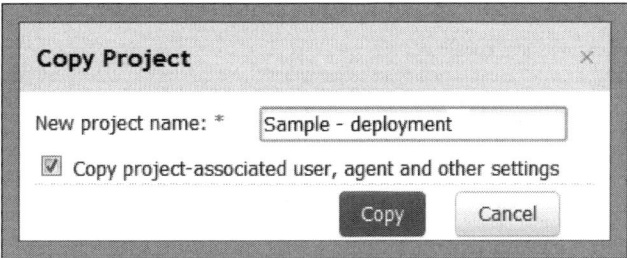

3. Enter a name for the new project and check the sole checkbox to copy every bit of settings from an original project—such as user settings, notifications, VCS roots, build agent, build configurations, and more. Click on **Copy** to submit your intent. Then you should see a confirmation message telling you that the project has been copied successfully. Project-associated settings were copied. Now go back to **Administration** | **Project-related Settings** | **Projects**.

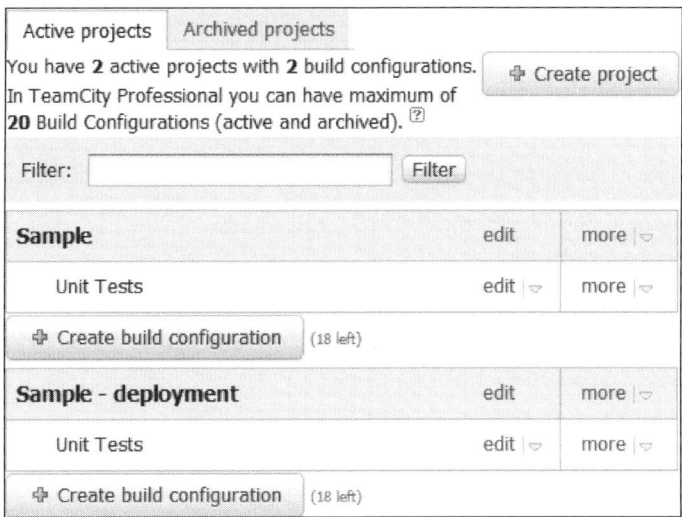

You can see now that there are two projects, and each of them has a build configuration called **Unit Tests,** looking very similar. These are two different configurations that just happen to share the same name and settings, as one has been copied from another.

Update build configurations

Let's customize this new build configuration.

1. In order to introduce different behavior for the `deployment` project, click on **edit** near its **Unit Tests** build configuration. Change the name relevantly (`Deploy WAR`) and save it by using the raised **Save** prompt. If you move to another step without saving the previous one, your changes will be lost. Go to **Build Step: Maven**. Add the following text into **Additional Maven command line parameters**:

    `-Dmaven.test.skip=true`

    This will instruct Maven not to run unit tests during this build step. Usually, for the deployment procedure, the test phase is omitted as all possible checks were already done using the dedicated **Unit Tests** build configurations and there's no reason to lengthen the process.

2. Save your changes now and let's go back to our original `Sample` TeamCity project and rename it with a new name, along with updating its build configuration for the tests to be launched, removing other commands related to further deployment process. We should do it as we've moved the latter into a separate build configuration. Click on **edit** near the **Sample** project name. Alter the existing name, add some description, and click on **Save**.

    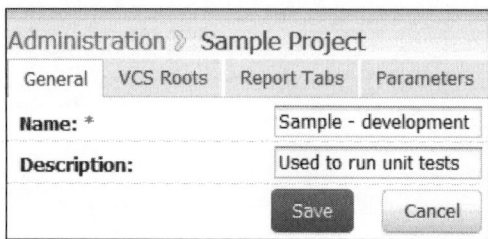

3. You should get a confirmation message saying that your changes have been saved. On the same page near the **edit** link, expand the menu with a down arrow and select **Build Step: Maven**. On the new screen, click on the **edit** link and replace the **install** goal with `test` in the **Goals** text field.

4. As soon as TeamCity detects that some part of the configuration has been changed, it will raise a warning prompt to let you save updates that are not yet saved. Click on **Save** and have your build step settings updated after seeing the corresponding confirmation box.

Extracting and applying a template

Let's imagine a possible situation where we need to have a **Unit Tests** build configuration in the `deployment` project too. This could be the outcome of the per-project restrictions when people who run the deployment procedure do not have access to the `development` project, but still want to make sure the build and tests are in good condition.

It is possible to make use of the already present build configuration:

1. We can extract the template from our existing **Unit Tests** build configuration. Go to **Administration** | **Project-related Settings** | **Projects** and click on the link **edit** near the **Unit Tests** build configuration. In the bottom-right corner, click on the **Extract Template** button.

2. Enter some meaningful name and hit the **Extract** button. You'll see a confirmation message saying **Build configuration template successfully created, build configuration is attached to the template**.

3. The template cannot be directly used across different projects. In order to use the template in another project, we need to move it there first. Go back to the **Sample – development** project settings, **Administration | Project-related Settings | Projects | Sample – development,** and click on our newly created template in the bottom-left corner, **Maven Unit Tests**. Now click on the **Move** button in the bottom-right corner of the page.

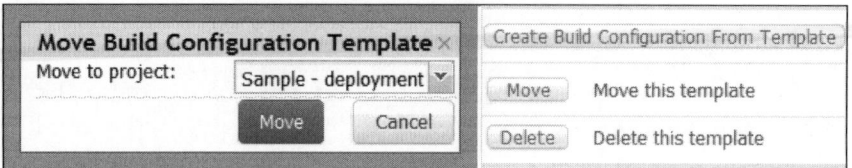

4. There's only one possible choice there; so, click on **Move**. Click on the **Create Build Configuration From Template** button in the bottom-right corner, enter the configuration name: Unit Tests from Template, and click on **Create**. A new build configuration will be immediately created based on the settings derived from the given template.

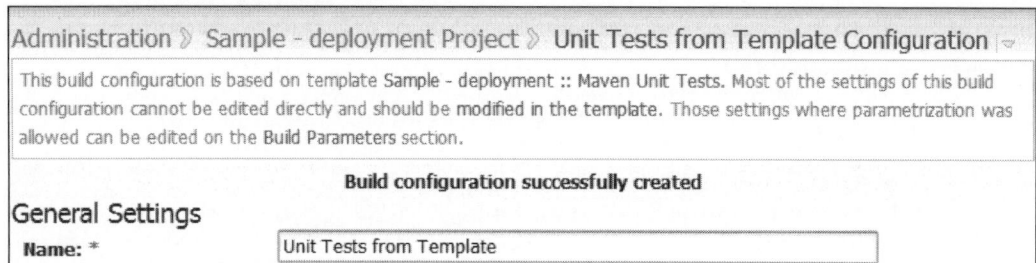

Multi-step builds

There are times when several inter-dependent steps need to be accomplished for a deployable artifact to be produced. TeamCity provides a flexible dependency sequence execution for related builds. We can create such multi-step builds based on our existing **Sample – deployment** project. The first step would be **Unit Tests from Template,** and the second one would be **Deploy WAR**.

Chapter 6

1. We need to create a new build configuration dependent on these two existing steps. Go to **Administration | Project-related Settings | Projects**. Click on the **Create Build Configuration** button under **Sample – deployment** project. Enter a name (Multi-Step Build) and click on **VCS Settings**. As this is the aggregation build, we don't need any particular interaction with the VCS here; so, just skip to next page by clicking on the **Add Build Step** button. The standard scenario for a build configuration creation requires going through these steps right until you reach the **Add Build Step** phase. You are not able to save your build configuration before that. You don't really have to change anything here now, so simply click on **Save**.

2. Now's the time when the configuration starts to get interesting. So far in this configuration, we have neither VCS settings nor any build steps. Let's add some dependencies here. On the right-hand side list of **Configuration Steps** click on **Dependencies**.

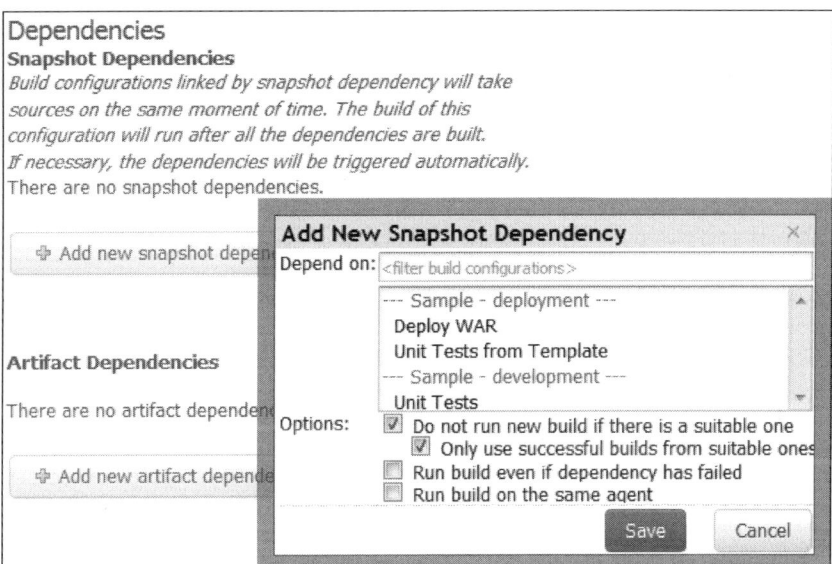

3. Here we have all the existing build configurations for all projects listed one-by-one. It is a good idea here to set the checkboxes as they are by default. Current settings mean that we will not trigger again any build we are depending on if that build is already up-to-date. But only those builds would be reused (and therefore not re-run) for which the results are successful. We may wish to go on even if some required dependency is broken, sometimes we have to. One more option we could ask for is the request that the build should be run on the same agent.

Enhanced Techniques

You are able to add the shown build configurations one by one or all at once. For the former approach, select **Unit Tests** from **Sample – development** and click on **Save**. You'll see that one dependency has been added to the previously empty list of snapshot dependencies. Now click on **Add new snapshot dependency** again but this time select the **Deploy WAR** configuration and click on **Save**. Otherwise, for the latter approach, press the *Ctrl* key and select both the configurations and hit **Save**.

Snapshot Dependencies			
☐ Depends on	Dependency options		
☐ Sample - deployment :: Deploy WAR	Do not run new build if there is a suitable one Only use successful builds from suitable ones	edit	delete
☐ Sample - development :: Unit Tests	Do not run new build if there is a suitable one Only use successful builds from suitable ones	edit	delete
➕ Add new snapshot dependency More Actions			

4. By now, you should already have two dependencies in the list. To add more realism into this story, we need to add a dependency of the Deploy WAR configuration on the `Unit Tests` build.

    i. To do so, go to **Administration | Project-related Settings | Projects | Sample - deployment**.

    ii. Then expand the drop-down menu near the **edit** link for the **Deploy WAR** configuration and select **Dependencies**.

    iii. Click on **Add new snapshot dependency** and select **Unit Tests**. That's it—you are done. Now let's go and check whether everything works out well for us.

    iv. Go to TeamCity's main page and click on **Run** near the **Multi-Step Build** build configuration.

In a few moments, TeamCity will enqueue in total three builds from the head build across all its dependencies.

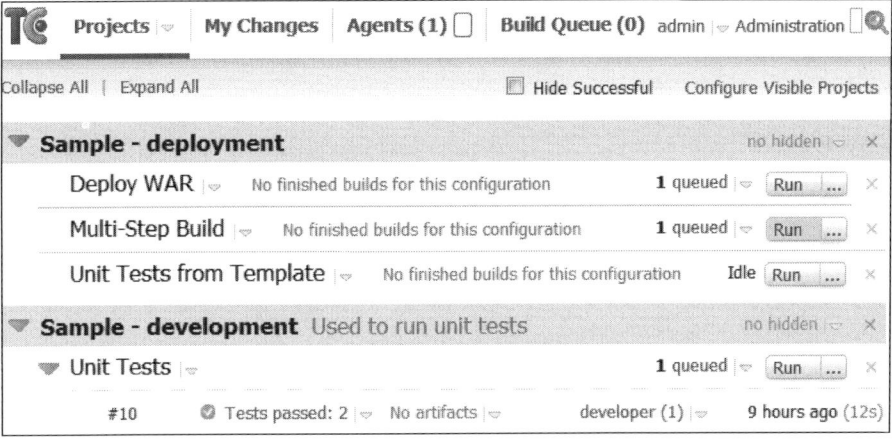

So we have the **Multi-Step Build** dependent both on **Deploy WAR** and on **Unit Tests** directly, along with a transitional dependency through the **Deploy WAR**'s dependency on **Unit Tests**.

Almost instantly, TeamCity starts the build chain in the proper order, and in a matter of seconds, the first **Multi-Step Build** instance is completed.

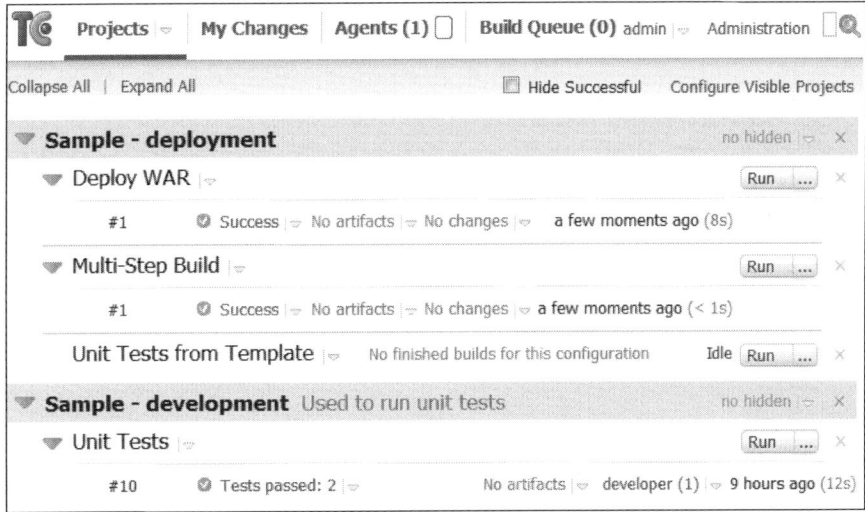

The timestamp of each build points out an interesting point. As we can see, TeamCity did not re-run the **Unit Tests** build even though it is stated as a required dependency both by **Multi-Step Build** and **Deploy WAR**. The reason is that there were no changes detected in the code since the last successful launch of this build, therefore, there's no need to execute it once again. The results of these builds were simply reused.

Deploy WAR in its turn was launched because it has never been executed ever before. It resulted in success, so by then both the dependencies were fine and **Multi-Step Build** could be finally run. Because in that build there were no more actions, it quickly moved to the succeeding state in less than a second, as is shown on the **Projects** overview page of TeamCity.

Summary

By the end of this chapter, you are informed of major advanced techniques you may use while working with TeamCity. Remote run being really one of the best amongst all, as it allows you to keep your source clean from simple mistakes or from code that does not pass tests and must not ever get to source control at all.

In the next chapter, you'll get information on the advanced configuration of TeamCity server. You'll know how to set up users and groups, and perform a backup and restore. Also you are going to upgrade the TeamCity server to the newer version, and learn how to use some advanced server settings.

7
Advanced Configuration

By now you should have a decent knowledge about TeamCity's major features and ways to configure them. Running Continuous Integration with TeamCity will not require you to know much. This chapter will describe some optional actions that may not be required very often; for example, performing backup and restore, or the addition of one more build agent. Though rarely used, these actions may come in handy for demanding software contributors. We'll get to know how it is possible to manage separate notifications for individual users and groups. After that, we will learn about an upgrade process for adding a backup and restore tool into our toolbox and finally install a supplementary build agent and assign it a particular build configuration.

In this chapter, you'll learn how to:

- Create users and groups
- Upgrade TeamCity to a newer version
- Manage the backup and restore process
- Install an additional build agent
- Assign an agent a particular build configuration

User and group notifications

We've already created these two users before:

- A chief admin user
- A more generic **developer** user

They both belong to a special **All Users** group containing all registered TeamCity users. This group is included in TeamCity by default and its name and description cannot be changed.

Advanced Configuration

Imagine that we need to have a separate group comprising of only developers and not QA engineers. Let's see how we can customize separate notification rules for different groups of users:

1. In order to add it, log in as an administrator and go to **Administration | User Management | Groups**. You will find a single group (as mentioned above).

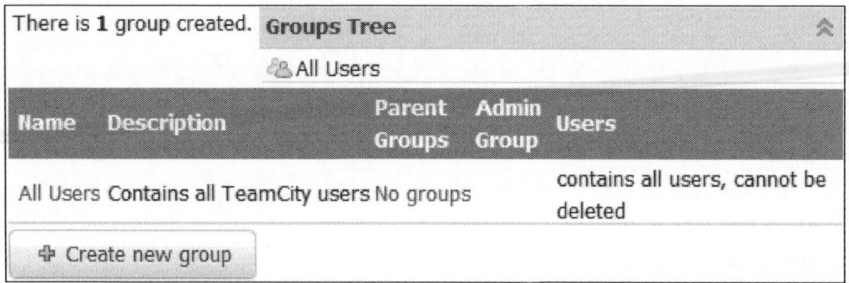

2. Now click on **Create new group**. Provide a relevant **Name** string, and a **Group Key** string will be generated automatically. If you want to inherit all notification settings and roles from some existing group—check the checkbox near the corresponding list item. As we need to create a distinct set of rules, leave the checkbox unchecked and click on the **Create** button.

3. You'll be brought back to the previous screen with some update stating that the group **Developers** has been created and has been made a top-level group as it does not have any parent. Now click on the name of the new group to edit its settings.

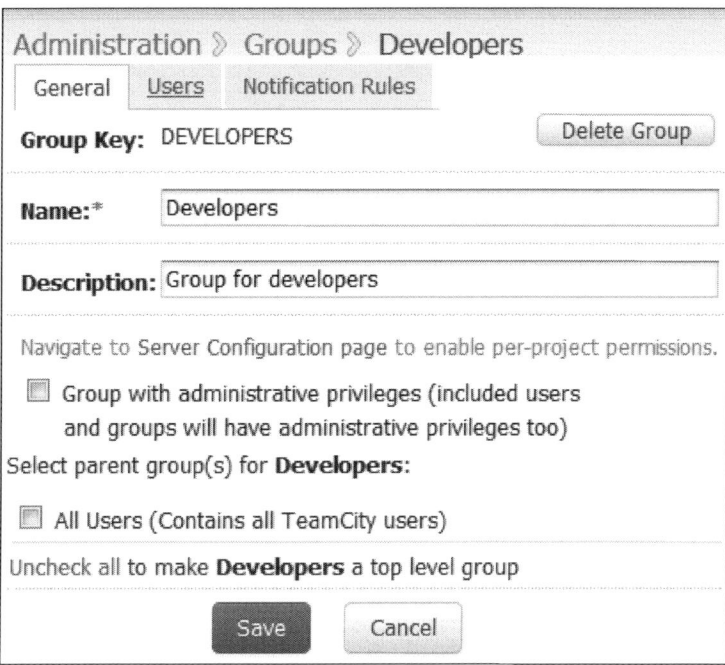

4. Group settings are presented with the following three tabs:
    ◦ The first tab is **General** and it contains some setting controls familiar to us from the group creation screen. But now one additional and interesting checkbox is available allowing us to force automatic administrative privilege assignment to all users included in this group. Also there is a link to **Server Configuration page** for quick access to enable per-project permissions.

Advanced Configuration

- ° The second tab is intended for showing the users that belong to the group, and as there is no such user yet the list is empty. There's a single button present on this page, **Add users to group**—let's click on it and add the user **developer** to this group.

Input `developer` into the search box and click on **Filter**. Select the single found entry and click on **Add to group**. You'll see a confirmation message saying **one user was successfully assigned to the group**. So as we are done with this tab, let's move over to the last one—**Notification Rules** and update the settings to later distinguish this group from the generic one.

- ° Go to the **Notification Rules** tab and click on **IDE notifier (0)**. As you may see we don't have any notifications set up for this group yet, because the group is new and does not extend any existing one which might have had some notifications configured.

  Click on the **Add new rule** button, select **Builds from the project | All projects** on the left and check all available checkboxes on the right. This will make it different from the previously configured generic rule in one setting. The new group will receive a notification for every build start which the **All Users** group won't.

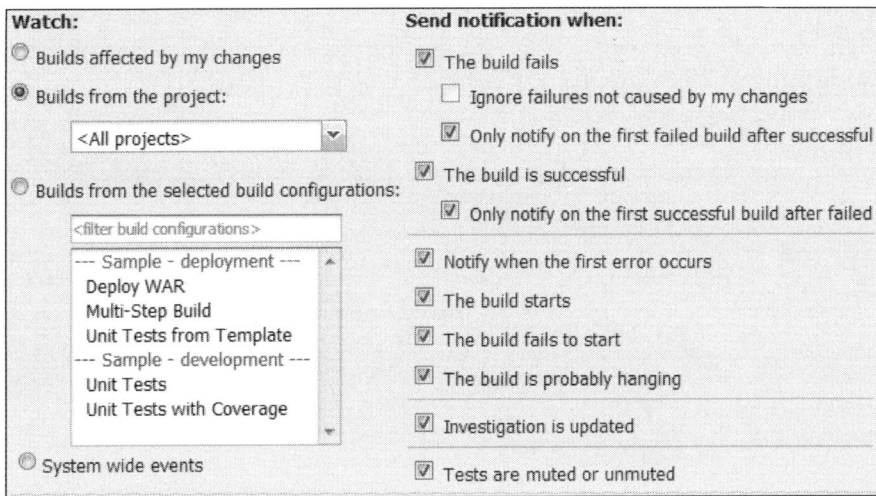

After clicking on **Save** you will receive a confirmation message **Notification rule added.**.

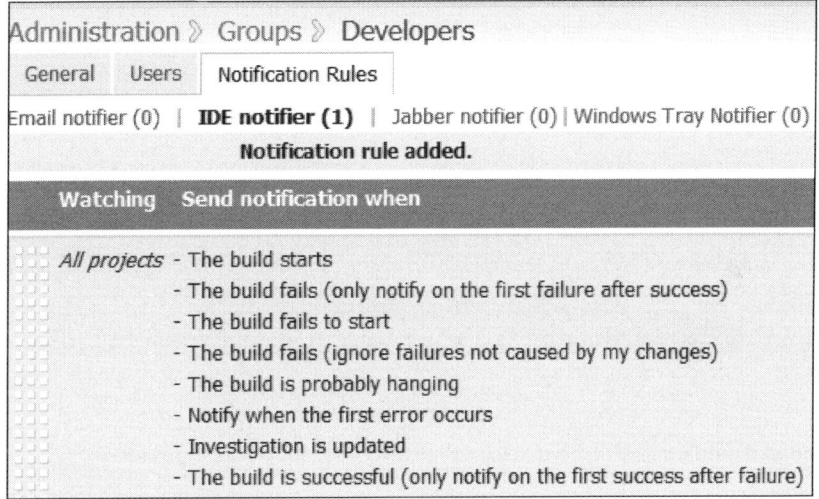

We can now verify that the two groups behave in a different way. This can be done via a simple test. As only the **developer** user is watching every build start and the user **admin** is not, we'll perform similar actions such as running a build via a web interface having been logged in as one and then another user and comparing what we see.

Advanced Configuration

5. In IDEA hover the mouse over the green check mark icon in the bottom-right corner and verify the tooltip message that says **You are logged in http://localhost as developer**.

   Now browse to `http://localhost` with your favorite browser and click on the **Run** button to the right of the **Unit Tests** build configuration underneath the **Sample – development** project, and keep an eye on the IDEA window. In a matter of seconds you are going to see an information tooltip window in IDEA.

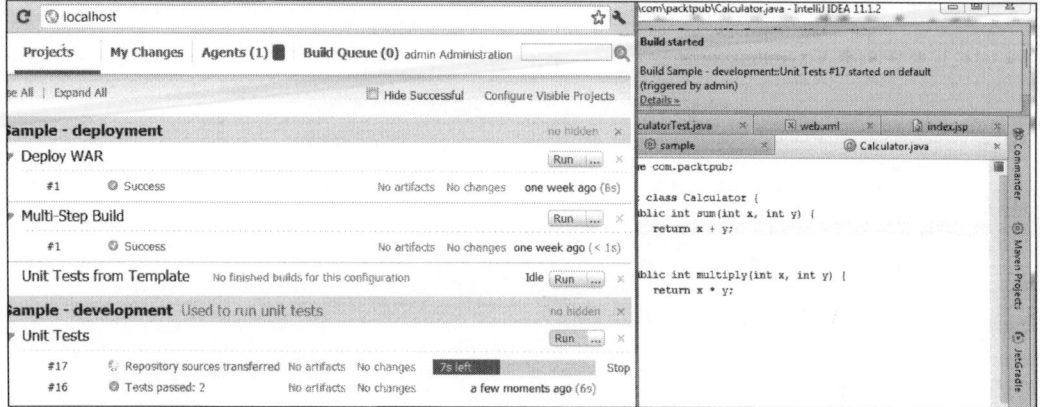

   From the message on the tooltip we can tell that **admin** has triggered a **Unit Tests** build either from the web interface or from the IDE plugin—the source of change does not matter. Now let's swap the current user with a different one.

6. In the IDEA menu go to **TeamCity | Logout** and then **TeamCity | Login**, and log in as `admin`.

7. Then again click on the **Run** button to the right of the **Unit Tests** build configuration underneath the **Sample – development** project in the web application.

8. You should not see the green tooltip in IDEA now, as compared to the previous try when you were logged in as **developer**.

Upgrading to a newer version

Time goes by and the latest version number of the software goes up. Each new patch brings some new bug fixes. Minor version updates add certain features while major version updates could carry total revamp of the whole application. Keeping up with the times proves useful, so updating the TeamCity server to a new version might come in handy.

In this section we shall do a backup first, then upgrade the TeamCity server to a newer version, and then restore its data back. Beware that there's one more situation where the backup/restore feature might be helpful. It is when you need to physically move the TeamCity server to another machine without losing all configuration and history details of the builds.

 There's no need to upgrade the build agents manually as they will be upgraded automatically after connecting to the upgraded server for the first time.

Backup

Before starting the upgrade process an experienced administrator should consider backing up the data for later restoring it into the newer version. Let's do a backup of TeamCity's data. There are three ways to sort that out:

- One, being suitable for regular maintenance backups, does this right from the web UI
- The second one is possible with the `maintainDB` command-line tool, which provides broader possibilities with fewer limitations than that from UI
- The last one is a full manual backup—the most powerful and the most tedious option

We shall go with the most straightforward generic one utilizing the web UI.

1. Browse the TeamCity web application and go to **Administration | Server Administration | Backup**.
2. Leave all the settings with default values and click on **Start Backup**. For a small database, the backup process will go fast and you'll get a backup report describing the location of the generated backup file and the timings for accomplished operation.

The last backup report	
Backup file:	D:\TeamCity\.Buildserver\backup\TeamCity_Backup_20120715_041630.zip (174.11Kb)
Preparing:	done in < 1s
Exporting database:	done in < 1s, exported 50 tables
Exporting settings and configurations:	done in 1s
Finishing:	done in < 1s
Backup completed successfully in 2s	

As a final check it would be good to verify that the generated file is not empty and then proceed with upgrading without worry.

Upgrading on Windows

It is very easy to find out if a new version is available because TeamCity has access to the Internet as it checks with Jetbrains' website for updates on a regular basis. Should TeamCity discover a newer version available, it starts showing an information hint in the footer right away.

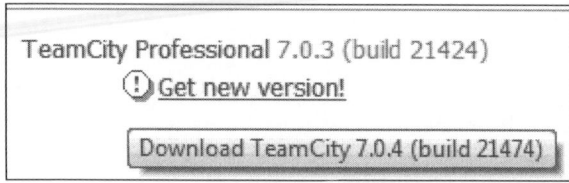

Also a corresponding warning box is present on every page in the **Administration** section.

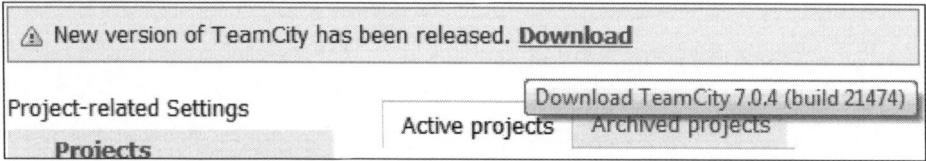

Click on the **Download** link and you will be redirected to the related web page. Select your operating system and click on **Download Now** to save the latest version on your hard drive.

Run the installer of the latest downloaded TeamCity version on the machine where TeamCity server resides. Select the same installation path with the current existing version of TeamCity and click on **Next**.

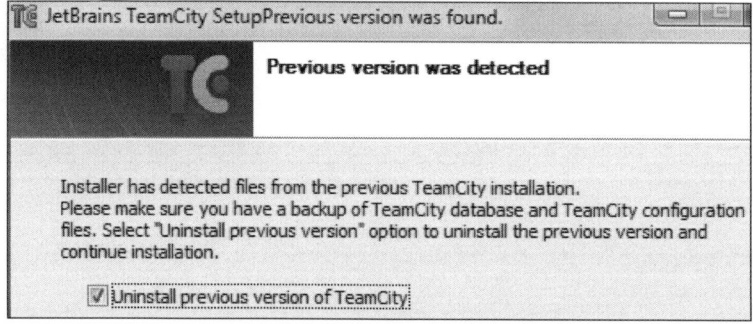

Uninstall the preceding version as this will give a clean installation with subsequent restoration of previously backed up data. In the next step you will be asked what data should be removed (such as logfiles and/or configuration files with the work directory). Selection of the proper options depends on the difference between the old and new version.

In case of an ordinary patch change you can safely keep all the data undeleted or for some reason you may wish to delete everything in case of huge version migration to restore data from the backup later. So uncheck all checkboxes and click on **Uninstall**. You can watch how the old version is being uninstalled and after completion you are going to be presented with a confirmation window. Click on **Finish** and proceed with the new version's installation.

Keep all the default settings which are taken from the previous installation and click on **Next** several times. Finally you'll see a build agent configuration's properties window depicting the agent's settings. As they match our preference, click on **Save**. Select the default build agent and TeamCity service options by clicking on **Next** several times and hit **Finish** at the end.

Upgrading on Linux

To perform an upgrade on Linux you can walk through these steps:

1. First you need to stop running the TeamCity server. Go to the `bin` directory under the TeamCity installation path, and run the following command:

    `/runAll.sh stop`

    This will stop both, the TeamCity server and the default build agent on the same machine (if any).

2. Remove the previous TeamCity installation directory (back it up first to be on the safe side). If you are using an external database or some additional plugins you will have to reinstall them after upgrade of the core server is finished.

3. Unpack the downloaded archive into the directory of the previous installation.

> Keeping all executable scripts in the same place as the one from the previous installation may be helpful if you are launching the TeamCity server during system startup.

4. In the `bin` directory under the TeamCity installation path run the following command:

   `/runAll.sh start`

5. This command will launch the TeamCity server and the default build agent if it is present on same machine. If you check the web interface you will see that after some time TeamCity fully initializes and becomes ready.

Restoring

If you now go to the main page of TeamCity, you'll see that the version at the bottom has changed to the latest one and there is no more indication of a newer version availability. As, in this example, we merely upgraded to the next patch version and during the uninstallation process we decided not to delete any data collected from the previous version, we can see that all our build settings, history of users' and groups' configuration is kept intact. However, sometimes such an easy update is not an option, so let's pretend we've deleted all the data and wish to restore previous data from backup. This is done via the `maintainDB` tool which resides in the `bin` folder underneath the TeamCity installation directory; for example, `d:\TeamCity\bin\maintainDB.cmd` on Windows or `.../TeamCity/bin/maintainDB.sh` on MacOS/Linux.

You need to make sure that the database and TeamCity data directory are both present and empty. Also you must stop TeamCity and then run the `maintainDB` tool with the `restore` option. The syntax for this execution is as follows:

```
maintainDB[cmd|sh] restore -F <full file name of TeamCity backup file>
-A <path to TeamCity Data Directory> -T <path to the database.properties
file of the target database>
```

For Windows installation use the command with a `.cmd` extension and for Linux use one with `.sh`.

That is all with restoring.

Advanced server settings

In this section we shall review some additional techniques such as installing an additional build agent and assigning it a dedicated build configuration.

Installing an additional build agent

Sometimes it is necessary to have particular build agents assigned to run specific builds. For instance, if your TeamCity server and default build agent are located on a Linux machine that is usually working in "headless" mode (without display), and you need to run tests for the Flex programming language, such as FlexUnit tests, then you will get into trouble. The bad thing here is that Flex classes should be placed on the "stage" to be accessed by tests, provided the default setup won't work. If you have limited access to that Linux machine you absolutely won't be able to run these tests there. A solution might not seem obvious in this situation, but all you need is a separate build agent on Windows machine. It will have a different build path and other running settings not the same. As you know, file paths in Linux and Windows are totally different and on Linux every path starts from the so-called *root* whereas on Windows there could be several logical disks such as C:\ and D:\. Build configurations which use path-sensitive settings will not work across platforms. So every other build being not the FlexUnit one might not work here.

Let's add one more build agent to the TeamCity server and assign it a particular configuration.

1. Go to **Administration** | **Project-related Settings** | **Projects** and on the right side of the page click on **Install Build Agents**.

    There are in total three installation variants as follows:

    - One is fully manual where you need to download and unpack the ZIP archive, and then customize the configuration by yourself in the buildAgent.properties file. Finally you need to physically launch this agent with scripts located in its \bin directory.
    - The next option is the MS Windows Installer instruction which is pretty similar to those we've used while installing a default agent together with the TeamCity server.
    - The last one is Java Web Start, which is a special technology that allows us to run Java applications directly from the Internet using a web browser.

Advanced Configuration

2. It would be useful to try Java Web Start for diversity's sake. So click on the corresponding link.

3. If you want to install a build agent into the machine where you've performed the download action, simply confirm that you want to run this application and select the preferred installation instructions' language on the next screen (that is, **English**). You will be welcomed with the installer window—click on **Next**. Select the destination directory and ensure that it exists; otherwise you'll get an error at this step.

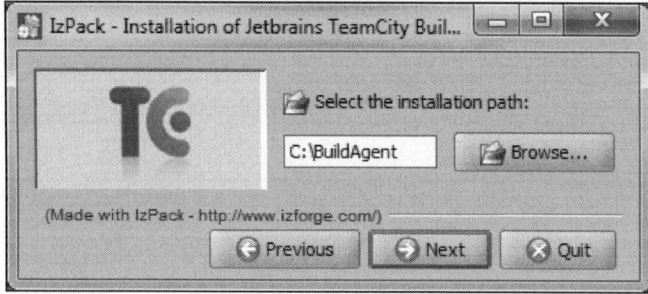

4. On the next screen uncheck the **Agent Windows Service** checkbox, as it is not possible to have more than one build agent of the same version working within a single Windows system.

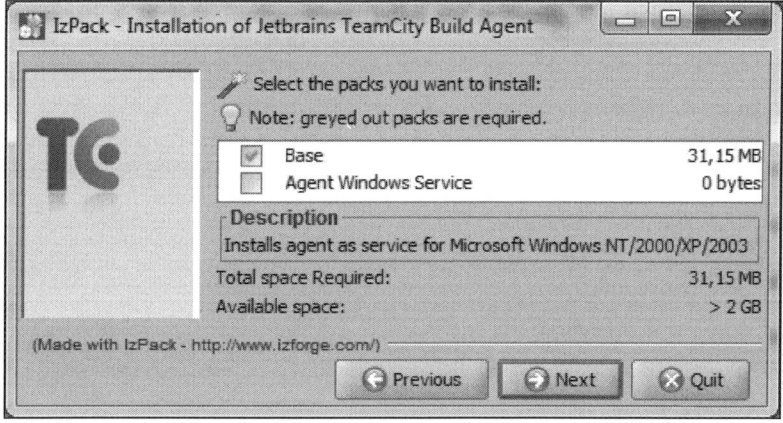

5. On the following screen confirm the settings and start the installation process by clicking on **Next**. Finally you are about to see the already familiar screen with build agent properties. Update the agent's name to distinguish it later among the others (Extra Agent), and set its port to any unused one in your system, such as 9999, and click on **Save**. Pay attention to the confirmation screen.

 By default, any new agent (except those installed on the same computer as TeamCity server) needs a special treatment to become capable of being used with TeamCity server.

6. Click on **Next** and then on **Done** in the installer window to complete the installation.

Start this new agent with the following command:

```
c:\BuildAgent\bin\agent.bat start
```

Advanced Configuration

A new command-line window will be opened. Wait for a few seconds for the agent to start fully. Moreover if the agent detects version incompatibility with the TeamCity server, it will automatically fetch the proper version from the server and start a self-upgrade all by itself.

When the start-and-upgrade process is finished you should see a message on the console like this:

```
Registered: id:3, authorizationToken:ed07ea973797b684451b189fc481fdbf
If this is the first time this agent registered on the server make sure it is au
thorized by administrator in the server web UI.
```

This means that the agent can connect to the TeamCity server and is ready to be authorized and enabled there. If you've installed an agent to the same machine that the server is installed onto, it will get authorized and enabled automatically. In a real world scenario it rarely makes sense to install two agents on one box, as they will fight against each other for system resources and will interfere with the server's own resource demands.

If you now browse to the **Agents** tab, you will merely see one single change from the previous appearance—one unauthorized agent has been added.

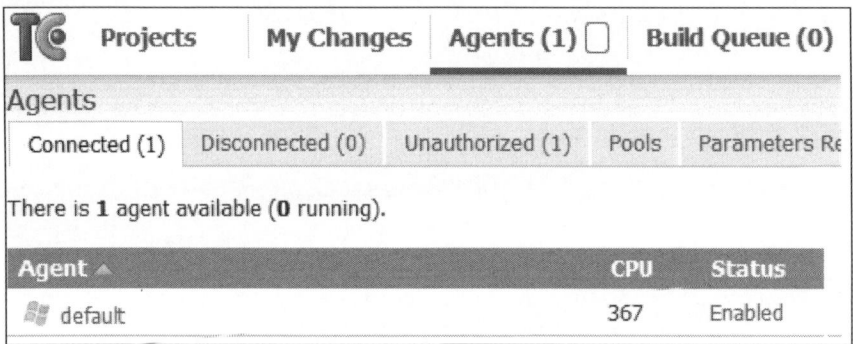

Click on the **Unauthorized** tab.

Here you can see that the TeamCity server has detected one unauthorized agent trying to connect from the IP address **192.168.1.192**. In order to authorize this agent, click on the **Unauthorized** link, enter a comment (or leave a default one in place), and select **Authorize**. Now this agent gets moved to the **Connected** tab.

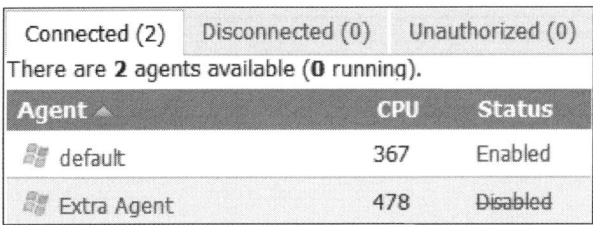

Open the Enable menu by clicking on the strike-through **Disabled** link and click on the **Enable** button. Now this new agent is completely ready for being utilized by the TeamCity server.

Assigning a dedicated build configuration

If you wish to attach build configuration to a particular agent:

1. Click on its name and go to the **Compatible Configurations** tab.
2. In the **Current run configuration policy** drop-down box select the **Run assigned configurations only** option, and assign specific configurations by clicking on the corresponding button, and check the necessary items in the list.

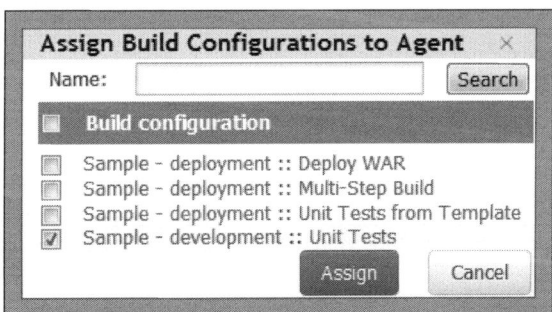

Advanced Configuration

3. Click on **Assign** and as a result you'll get a certain build configuration assigned to its dedicated build agent.

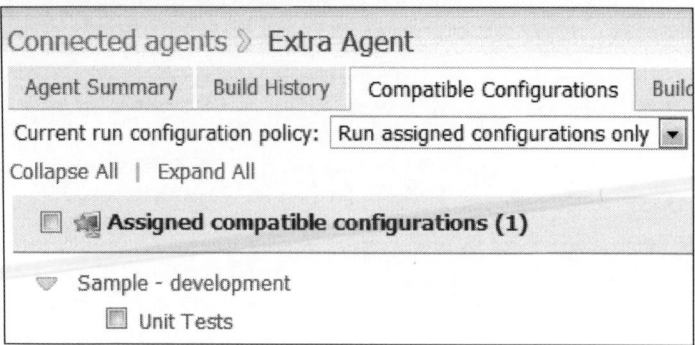

Summary

In this chapter we have learned how to work with users and groups in TeamCity. Also we performed backup and restore procedures that may help a lot when there is a need to move the TeamCity server to another machine. Next we've learned how to perform an upgrade to a newer version and finally reviewed the installation of a new build agent and the steps needed to assign it a particular build configuration.

Where to Go Next

No single book might be big enough to cover all required applications for Continuous Integration and the vast possibilities of TeamCity. There is still lots and lots of information that the user could find useful, including integration with powerful code inspection tools such as Sonar or issue management systems such as JIRA. It is possible to maintain the full project lifecycle starting from running basic "smoke" unit tests, followed up by integration and regression tests, up to the final production deployment with uses of TeamCity.

However the amount of information that we've managed to go through here is enough to start applying CI from scratch and keep continuously evolving it to meet your needs. So far we have learned:

- What TeamCity is, why it is worth attention, and its terms and concepts.
- How to create a simple project that could benefit from Continuous Integration. We've used Maven for source-code generation, written some unit tests, and committed all this into the version control system.
- Ways to install and launch TeamCity server and its default build agent.
- Basic configuration possibilities to start using TeamCity, ways to work with projects and build configurations, creating users, and configuring their notifications.
- How to integrate TeamCity into two popular IDEs, namely IntelliJ IDEA and Eclipse.
- How to make your project safer with remote runs, more convenient with templates, and smarter with multi-step builds.
- Finally, we've had a good look at how to manage advanced notification options for users and groups, steps required to back up and restore your data collected by TeamCity, and the means to install additional build agents into the TeamCity server.

- I hope this book helps you with starting to utilize the powers of Continuous Integration by means of TeamCity. Everything that is needed for a good start and consequent look at the right direction should be provided here. The more you know about TeamCity, the easier it gets to apply it according to your demands and receive all benefits of applying Continuous Integration. Links which could be useful for further learning are listed as follows:
- The priceless source of information about every version of TeamCity can be found on the related Jetbrains website at `http://www.jetbrains.com/teamcity/`. From here you will be able to get a brief overview of TeamCity, read about features and what's new, and download the TeamCity installation bundle and/or plugins. All information concerning licensing and upgrading can be also found here.
- A link to the online reference of the latest (currently) seventh version is `http://confluence.jetbrains.net/display/TCD7/TeamCity+Documentation`. Here you can find almost everything about TeamCity starting from the *Getting Started* tutorial, up to instructions on extending TeamCity by written plugins.
- Don't miss the community forum for TeamCity located at `http://devnet.jetbrains.net/community/teamcity` and also an official TeamCity blog where you can find all the news on new version releases or some outstanding events related to TeamCity: `http://blogs.jetbrains.com/teamcity/`.
- Should you find some bug in TeamCity or wish to request a certain new function, please use their issue tracking system at: `http://youtrack.jetbrains.com/issues/TW`.

All I can do now is wish you good luck with your current and future ventures. I hope this book will help your projects to be rock solid and prevent any unexpected and unwelcome surprises, such as uncompilable code in the main trunk or a sudden discovery of a failing test ahead of tomorrow's release to production. All of this comes along with a confidence in the steadiness of the development process utilizing the power of Continuous Integration provided by means of TeamCity.

Index

A

additional build agent
  installing 103-107
advanced configuration, TeamCity server
  advanced server settings 102
  upgrading, to new version 98
  user and group notifications 93
advanced server settings
  additional build agent, installing 103-107
  dedicated build configuration, assigning to agent 107
agent-side checkout, VCS 16
application
  launching 32, 33
architecture, TeamCity 14
arguments, command line
  -DachetypeArtifactId 23
  -DachetypeGroupId 23
  -DartifactId 23
  -DgroupId 23
  -DinteractiveMode 23
  -Dversion 23
  archetype:generate 23
Atom/RSS feed notifier
  configuring 63
automatic build triggering
  setting up 8

B

backup, TeamCity server 99
build agent
  about 10, 11, 35
  default build agent, installing 42-44
  installing 42
build artifact 11, 16
build configuration
  about 11
  creating 50, 51
  running 52
  triggering automatically 53-57
build lifecycle
  about 14
  build agent, scheduling to 15
  build, running 16
  VCS specifics 16

C

ClearCase 13
code coverage
  about 12
  URL 12
community forum
  reference link 110
concepts, TeamCity
  about 10
  build agent 10, 11
  build artifacts 11
  build configuration 11
  code coverage 12
  My changes 12
  notifiers 13
  pre-tested commit (remote run) 13
  project 13
  VCS 13
Continuous Integration 8
custom notification rules
  adding 63, 64
CVS 13

D

dedicated build configuration
  assigning, to agent 107
default build agent
  installing 43, 44
development environment
  creating 20
  JDK, installing 20
  Maven, installing 22
  Windows environment, configuring 20-22

E

Eclipse
  TeamCity plugin, installing 70-72
e-mail notifier
  configuring 62
enhanced techniques, TeamCity
  multiple projects, organizing with templates 84
  multi-step builds, creating 88
  remote run, performing 73, 74

F

features, TeamCity. *See* **TeamCity features**

G

Git 13

H

hardware requisites, TeamCity
  build agent 35
  server 36

I

IDE 19
IDE notifier
  configuring 62
installing
  build agent 42
  Linux multi-platform distribution 39-41
  TeamCity server 37
  Windows distribution 37-39

integration, TeamCity server configuration 58
IntelliJ IDEA
  about 65
  installing 24
  installing, from TeamCity server 66, 67
  sample project, opening with 24-28
  TeamCity plugin, installing 68-70
  TeamCity plugin, installing from plugins repository 66
issue tracking system
  reference link 110

J

Jabber 9
Jabber/XMPP notifier
  configuring 63
JDK
  about 19
  installing 20
Jetbrains 36
JIRA 109

L

Linux
  TeamCity server, upgrading 101
Linux multi-platform distribution, TeamCity server
  installing 39, 41

M

Maven
  about 19
  installing 22
Mercurial 13
multiple projects, with templates
  build configurations, updating 86, 87
  creating 84
  project, copying 84, 85
  template, applying 88
  template, extracting 87, 88
multi-step builds
  creating 88-92
my changes 12

N

notifications, TeamCity server
  Atom/RSS feed 63
  custom notification rules, adding 63, 64
  e-mail 62
  IDE 62
  Jabber/XMPP 63
  preinstalled configurations 63
  Windows tray 62
notifier 13

P

Perforce 13
prerequisites, TeamCity server configuration 47
pre-tested commit 13
project
  about 13
  committing, to Subversion 48, 49
  creating 49
project-related settings, TeamCity server configuration 57

Q

quiet period 10

R

remote run
  about 73
  working 73, 74
  working, in Eclipse 80-83
  working, in IntelliJ IDEA 75-79
restoring, TeamCity server 102
RSS feeds 9

S

sample project
  creating 23
  IntelliJ IDEA, installing 24
  opening, with IDEA 24-28
  source, generating by Maven 23, 24
server administration, TeamCity server configuration
  about 58
  Agent Cloud page 59
  Diagnostics page 59
  Global settings page 58
  Licenses page 59
  Usage Statistics page 59
server-side checkout, VCS 16
SourceGear Vault 13
StarTeam 13
Subversion 13
SVN server
  setting up 47

T

TeamCity
  about 7
  architecture 14
  build configuration, creating 50
  build lifecycle 14
  download link 35
  enhanced techniques 73
  features 8
  hardware requisites 35
  project, creating 49
  terms and concepts 10
TeamCity bundle 37
TeamCity community forum
  reference link 110
TeamCity features
  about 8
  advanced features 10
  automatic build triggering 8
  code coverage 9
  comprehensive build infrastructure 9
  configurable test reports 9
  easy to verify code changes 9
  enhanced VCS integration 10
  inspections 9
  instant notifications 9
  manual build triggering 8
  pre-tested commit 9
TeamCity issue tracking system
  reference link 110
TeamCity online administration guide
  URL 57

TeamCity plugin
  installing, into Eclipse 70-72
  installing, into IntelliJ IDEA 66-69
TeamCity server
  advanced configuration 93
  configuring 47, 57
  installing 37
  notifications, configuring 62
  running 44-46
  users, maintaining 59
  users permissions, maintaining 60, 61
TeamCity server configuration
  integration 58
  prerequisites 47
  project-related settings 57
  server administration 58
TeamCity server installation
  about 37
  from WAR archive 42
  Linux multi-platform distribution,
      installing 39-41
  Windows distribution, installing 37-39
TeamCity server, upgrade
  about 99
  backup 99
  restoring 102
  upgrading on Linux 101
  upgrading on Windows 100, 101
TeamCity seventh version
  reference link 110
TeamCity versions
  reference link 110
Team Foundation Server 13
testSum() method 31

U

unit tests
  adding 29
  first test, writing 30, 31
  testable code, creating 29
upgrade process, TeamCity server. *See*
  TeamCity server, upgrade
user and group notifications
  customizing 93-98
users permissions, TeamCity server
  maintaining 61
users, TeamCity server
  maintaining 59

V

VCS
  about 13
  ClearCase 13
  CVS 13
  Git 13
  Mercurial 13
  Perforce 13
  SourceGear Vault 13
  StarTeam 13
  Subversion 13
  Team Foundation Server 13
  Visual SourceSafe 13
VCS configuration 10
VCS specifics, build lifecycle
  agent-side checkout 16
  server-side checkout 16
Version Control System. *See* **VCS**
Visual SourceSafe 13
Visual SVN server
  URL 47

W

WAR archive
  Teamcity server, installing from 42
Windows
  TeamCity server, upgrading 100, 101
Windows distribution, TeamCity server
  installing 37-39
Windows environment
  configuring 20, 21
Windows system tray notifier
  configuring 62

Thank you for buying
TeamCity 7 Continuous Integration Essentials

About Packt Publishing

Packt, pronounced 'packed', published its first book "*Mastering phpMyAdmin for Effective MySQL Management*" in April 2004 and subsequently continued to specialize in publishing highly focused books on specific technologies and solutions.

Our books and publications share the experiences of your fellow IT professionals in adapting and customizing today's systems, applications, and frameworks. Our solution based books give you the knowledge and power to customize the software and technologies you're using to get the job done. Packt books are more specific and less general than the IT books you have seen in the past. Our unique business model allows us to bring you more focused information, giving you more of what you need to know, and less of what you don't.

Packt is a modern, yet unique publishing company, which focuses on producing quality, cutting-edge books for communities of developers, administrators, and newbies alike. For more information, please visit our website: www.packtpub.com.

About Packt Open Source

In 2010, Packt launched two new brands, Packt Open Source and Packt Enterprise, in order to continue its focus on specialization. This book is part of the Packt Open Source brand, home to books published on software built around Open Source licences, and offering information to anybody from advanced developers to budding web designers. The Open Source brand also runs Packt's Open Source Royalty Scheme, by which Packt gives a royalty to each Open Source project about whose software a book is sold.

Writing for Packt

We welcome all inquiries from people who are interested in authoring. Book proposals should be sent to author@packtpub.com. If your book idea is still at an early stage and you would like to discuss it first before writing a formal book proposal, contact us; one of our commissioning editors will get in touch with you.

We're not just looking for published authors; if you have strong technical skills but no writing experience, our experienced editors can help you develop a writing career, or simply get some additional reward for your expertise.

Agile IT Security Implementation Methodology

ISBN: 978-1-849685-70-2 Paperback: 120 pages

Plan, develop, and execute your organization's robust agile security with IBM's Senior IT Specialist

1. Combine the Agile software development best practices with IT security practices to produce incredible results and minimize costs

2. Plan effective Agile IT security using mind mapping techniques

3. Create an Agile blueprint and build a threat model for high value asset

Jenkins Continuous Integration Cookbook

ISBN: 978-1-849517-40-9 Paperback: 344 pages

Over 80 recipes to maintain, secure, communicate, test, build, and improve the software development process with Jenkins

1. Explore the use of more than 40 best of breed plugins

2. Use code quality metrics, integration testing through functional and performance testing to measure the quality of your software

3. Get a problem-solution approach enriched with code examples for practical and easy comprehension

Please check www.PacktPub.com for information on our titles

Python Testing Cookbook

ISBN: 978-1-849514-66-8   Paperback: 364 pages

Over 70 simple but incredibly effective recipes for taking control of automated testing using powerful Python testing tools

1. Learn to write tests at every level using a variety of Python testing tools

2. The first book to include detailed screenshots and recipes for using Jenkins continuous integration server (formerly known as Hudson)

3. Explore innovative ways to introduce automated testing to legacy systems

4. Written by Greg L. Turnquist – senior software engineer and author of Spring Python 1.1

Web Services Testing with soapUI

ISBN: 978-1-849515-66-5   Paperback: 332 pages

Build high quality service-oriented solutions by learning easy and efficient web services testing with this practical, hands-on guide.

1. Become more proficient in testing web services included in your service-oriented solutions

2. Find, analyze, reproduce bugs effectively by adhering to best web service testing approaches

3. Learn with clear step-by-step instructions and hands-on examples on various topics related to web services testing using soapUI

Please check **www.PacktPub.com** for information on our titles

Printed in Great Britain
by Amazon.co.uk, Ltd.,
Marston Gate.